PREFACE

Many friends have expressed the desire to have a book printed which gives religious anecdotes, etc., suitable for young readers. To meet their wish this book is issued by the Publications Committee of the Free Presbyterian Church of Scotland, with the prayer that it will be abundantly blessed to many.

W. GRANT,

Convener.

August, 1961   **Halkirk, Caithness.**

Reprinted May 1963

Free Presbyterian Church of Scotland

ISSUED BY

THE PUBLICATIONS COMMITTEE

" Thou hast given a banner to them that fear Thee that it may be displayed because of the truth."

Ps. LX. 4.

To Neil Matheson

From Lochcarron Free Church
Sabbath School

June 1982.

CONTENTS

CHILDREN'S TREASURY

A THREEFOLD CORD

No. I.

Precept.—Suffer the little children to come unto me, and forbid them not; for of such is the kingdom of God.   Mark x. 14.

Promise.—Him that cometh to me I will in no wise cast out.   John vi. 37.

Prayer.—Draw me, we will run after thee. Song of Sol. i. 4.

When God gives us a *precept*, or command, in his word, we will always find that he gives us a *promise* also, to encourage us to obey.   And we shall often find a *prayer*, just suited to the precept and promise.   Try to take these three-fold cords *together*, dear children, and so, when you have to obey any precept, you will be able to remember the promise, and ask for help in the prayer.

Ask the Lord, by his Holy Spirit, to draw you to himself, and help you to keep always near him in the narrow way.   And do not go alone, but try to bring others with you.

SEEKING EARLY

An old man one day took a child on his knee, and talked to him about Jesus, and told him to seek the Saviour now, and pray to him and love him. The child knew that the old man was not himself a Christian, and felt surprised.   Then he looked up into the old man's face and said,   " But why don't *you* seek God ?"

The old man was affected by the question, and replied, " Ah, my dear child !   I neglected to do so when I was young, and now my heart is so hard that I fear I never shall be able."

Ah, my reader ! believe him.   " To-day, if ye will hear his voice, harden not your hearts." It will be more difficult to hear to-morrow.   And weeks, and months, and years hence, even could you be sure of them, how high and strong a barrier will gradually be rising between you and Christ ! " They that seek me *early* shall find me."

A SABBATH WELL SPENT

A Sabbath well spent
Brings a week of content,
And health for the toils of to-morrow,
But a Sabbath profaned,
Whatso'er may be gained
Is a certain forerunner of Sorrow.

THE LORD'S MY SHEPHERD

The Lord's my shepherd, I'll not want.
　He makes me down to lie,
In pastures green: he leadeth me
　the quiet waters by.

My soul he doth restore again;
　and me to walk doth make
Within the paths of righteousness,
　ev'n for his own name's sake.

Yea, though I walk in death's dark vale,
　yet will I fear none ill:
For thou art with me; and thy rod
　and staff me comfort still.

My table thou hast furnished
　in presence of my foes;
My head thou dost with oil anoint,
　and my cup overflows.

Goodness and mercy all my life
　shall surely follow me:
And in God's house for evermore
　my dwelling-place shall be.

　　　　　　　　—Psalm 23.

A SABBATH-LOVING RED INDIAN

Many years ago, a mission was established among the Wyandot Indians, then occupying a part of the country in Huron county, Ohio, America. A company of converted Indians had left the Reservation, and established themselves on White River for a winter's hunt.   It was soon rumoured abroad that there were religious Indians there, and many of the white people, led by curiosity, went to attend their meetings on Sabbath days.   Frequent attempts were made to turn the Indians from the observance of the Christian rule of duty, and especially from the observance of the Sabbath, but without success.

A company of white people came one Sabbath, and insisted on trading.   The leader of the Indians, whose name was " Between-the-logs " went to his saddle bag, and pulled out his Bible. He could not read it, yet he was in the habit of saying it was good company, even if a man could not read it, to have the Word of God with him, and perhaps he could get some one to read it for him. He had marked the Chapter, which contained the Ten Commandments.   He opened at the place and asked one of the men if he could read, handing him the Book.   At this the man turned pale, and did not wish to touch it, but, at the earnest request of the other, read the Fourth Commandment.

" Now," said the Indian chief, " you white men have read this Book all your lives, and are taught to read it and understand that you must keep God's Day holy. Here are you trying not only to break this law of God, but to get us poor Indians to do so too. Of this you ought to be ashamed and never do so again. Your example to your families and friends is bad; and you will have a great deal to answer for at God's judgment-seat if you keep on in this course. Now we wish you and all your friends to know that we have learned better. When we were in the dark we did not know better; but the light of Heaven has shone on our path, and it has shown us that it is good for our souls, and our bodies, and our horses, and all, that we should stop one day in seven and think, and pray, and look to our hearts to untie them from the things of this world—for they are naturally much inclined to stick fast to this world. God saw it was best to take one day to loosen them and keep them right. If this is not done, they will soon grow fast. Then nothing will do but tearing, and this is hard work. I believe God is right, and that He has done it for the good of us all; and we ought to keep His good Word, so that it may be well with us. I am told that this Book of His says, if we do not keep His Commandments, we shall never enter His house above. My white brothers, go home and never go to trade again on the Sabbath, God's holy Day. You will find it better with you in this world, and also in the world to come.''

MUCKLE KATE

(A Trophy of Grace)

Among the Highlanders of Ross-shire the name of Mr Lachlan MacKenzie, the godly minister of Lochcarron, was very fragrant, and even now there may be some to whom " the great Mr Lachlan " is a pleasant name.

The following story will illustrate the sovereignty and power of grace, and is given on the authority of a late eminent, godly minister in Ross, who was an eye-witness of the principal scenes herein stated.

Not far from the manse of Lochcarron a wicked, old sinner lived, who was supposed to have been guilty of every forbidden crime in the Law of God except murder. As she had very masculine dimensions she was known as " Muckle Kate." " An ill-looking woman without any beauty in the sight of God and man," Mr Lachlan used to say of her. The efforts of her Minister could not succeed to get from her even occasional attendance at the House of God ; entreaties, visits, appeals to her conscience many and strong were made by him, but all in vain ; nothing could reach the heart which seemed certainly to have reached the point " past feeling." Her Minister adopted a plan to reach her conscience, which certainly was very strange ; some would, perhaps, say it was unwarrantable, but God owned it, and as He is a Sovereign, doing just

as He will, we shall not say " it was unwarrantable."   It was customary among the Highlanders,
during the last century, to meet at nightfall in each
other's houses, and spend the long evening in
singing Gaelic melodies.   The women brought with
them their distaffs and spindles, while the men
mended their brogues or weaved baskets and creels.
This was called " going on kailie."

Kate devoted herself to this practice with
eagerness.   Her Minister knowing this, and having
a turn for rhyming, composed a Gaelic song in
which all Kate's known sins were enumerated and
lashed with all the severity of which the composer
was capable.   This song Mr Lachlan set to music,
and sending for some persons who were known to
" go on kailie " with Kate he taught them the
song and instructed them to sing it in her hearing
on the first opportunity.   Strange! It was so,
but the suddenness of the blow, from such an unexpected quarter, gave point to the stroke, while
God drove the truth right home to her heart.

Her agony of mind was fearful.   The bleak
scenery of Lochcarron was in strange unison with
her feelings.   Among the dreary mountains of that
lonesome, western wilderness runs up the small es-
tuary from which the parish derives its name.   In
these wilds Kate now spent most of her time.   For
what purpose ? Joseph-like, she sought where to
weep.   The solitudes of Lochcarron were heard to
resound with the voice of wailing, and the inmates

of the bothies amid the hills knew from whose lips those cries of agony were wrung.   They came from the once hardened Muckle Kate.   Deep as her conviction was, it never seemed to subside; weeks, months, even years passed, yet the sorrows of the convicted sinner were as fresh as ever.   " Never breathed a wretch like her; there might be hope for others, but oh, there was none for Muckle Kate !"

She was a " wonder to many," as well she might be, for at her age, between 80 and 90, it is rare to see a person called by grace.   However, age has nothing to do with the matter as in God's sight; the set time had come for her to be brought to know herself a sinner, and now she was a wonder to her neighbours, to unbelievers, to the Church, to her astonished Minister, but most of all a wonder to herself.   Into the depths of conviction under the Law she, poor soul, went, inasmuch as to understand that part of it which says: " I also will do this unto you: I will even appoint cver you terror, consumption, and the burning ague, that shall consume the eyes " (Lev. 26: 16), and Muckle Kate wept herself stone blind !   Yes, without exaggerating by a hair's-breadth, she wept away her eyesight !   Poor Kate !   Rich Kate ! !   What deep, penetrating eyes she had into her own soul's state before God ! ! !   Would that God would give many of us in this hard-hearted day a few tears for sin.

During one of her visits to the manse, and while waiting to converse with her Minister, she heard the noise of a flock of ducklings, and, not aware of the presence of any other person, she said, " O, my poor things, ye're happy, happy creatures. Ye ha'e na' crucified a Saviour like me ; it would be well for Muckle Kate to be a duck like you, for then she would have no sin to answer for—no sin, no sin !" Others have entered a little into this feeling of the poor, blind woman. In the third year of her sorrow for sin her Minister was anxious for her to sit down at the Lord's Table, but nothing could prevail upon her to comply with his requests.

" I go forward to that holy table ! I, who have had my arms up to the shoulders in a Saviour's blood ! My presence would profane that blessed ordinance, and would be enough to pollute the whole congregation ! Never will I sit down at that Table ; the Communion is not for me !" However, it was for her. The Communion day arrived, the hour of meeting drew nigh, but Kate's determination still remained unchanged. The Tables had all been served, the elements removed, the Minister had returned to " the tent," and all were listening for the words of the concluding address, when a cry of despair was heard in a distant part of the audience—a shriek of female agony—that rose loud and clear, and was returned, as if in sympathy, by the echoes of the surrounding hills. It was the voice of Muckle Kate, who now thought all was over. Hundreds started to their feet and looked

anxiously toward the spot whence the scream had
proceeded.   Mr Lachlan knew the voice, and as
each true pastor has a pastor's heart, he understood
the cause of the cry, stepped over among the
people till he had reached the spot, took Kate
kindly by the hand, led her through the crowd to
the Communion Table, and seated her at the head.
He next ordered the elements to be brought forward and replaced upon the Table ; and there sat
that one solitary, blind being, alone in the midst
of thousands — every eye of the vast multitude
turned in wonder upon her—partaking of the em-
blems of the Saviour's body and blood, and she herself unconscious of their gaze.   Mr Lachlan spoke
from the words—" Not a hoof of them shall be
left," and his address was so blessed to the
assembled multitude that it is computed that two
hundred were awakened to a sense of their lost
estate.

Muckle Kate lived about three years after this,
manifesting the marks of a close and humble walk
with God.   Not having seen any account as to the
manner of her Gospel deliverance from the terrors
of the Law under which she so long suffered, we
cannot state the means used, but of the reality of
her deliverance, her life henceforth, and her
triumphant death testify.   As Muckle Kate was led
deep into the knowledge of sin and sorrow for sin,
so she was led deep into the knowledge of Christ ;
and so clear as to her interest in His work, that
assurance became so sure that she ceased to think of
self ; she was absorbed in the glory of her Re-

deemer, Christ was " all in all " to her.   " For as
the sufferings of Christ abound in us, so our consolation also aboundeth by Christ," was her happy
experience.

As she stood on the threshold of eternal glory,
her sanctified tongue was heard to exclaim, as its
farewell effort to honour Christ :   " Tell, tell to
others that I have found him."   Lay the emphasis
upon the ' I ' and what depth of sin, shame and
pollution are comprised in that ' I.'   If we could
compress into that ' I ' those ninety years of sin—
as she had been taught sin—as she had felt sin—
as she had wept her sight away for sin—we should
better catch what she meant when she said, " *I*
have found Him."

" Tell them that the worst of sinners—the
drunkard, the profligate, the Sabbath-breaker, the
thief, the blasphemer, the liar, the scoffer, the in-
fidel — tell them that I, a living embodiment of
every sin, even I, have found a Saviour's person,
even I have known a Saviour's love."

" This is a faithful saying, and worthy of all
acceptation, that Christ Jesus came into the world
to save sinners, of whom I am chief."

Reader, if you fear God, you will bless Him
for such mercy as is here evident.   But if one reads
this who is still without God, I would say : you may
not have sinned openly as poor Muckle Kate, but
God looks on your heart, and unless you partake

of saving mercy before you die, you must be eternally lost.   Hell is solemnly true, notwithstanding
many declaring against it.   The wages of sin is
death—eternal death—after the death of the body.
Should a true seeker read this, one who feels he is
too bad for salvation, surely here is something to
encourage such to hope for mercy.   If He has given
you the felt want, the anxious yearning after His
blood to be applied to your soul ; if He, in mercy,
has granted you sorrow for sin, then it is hoped,
by His blessing, that this record of saving mercy
may encourage you to press your case before Him
Who is " plenteous in mercy."

NARRATIVES OF MISSION LIFE
IN RHODESIA

—By Rev. John Tallach

It is of the very spirit of a mission report to include some record of these goings of our King, and we will at least have done something, if we can make you experience part of that joy felt by ourselves so often during the year.

Here, for instance, is Sibonile, her body now in its shrinking stage through old age.   She cannot remember when she began to take drink.   And she was unashamed with it, too, for would she not lie drunk in the company while the Missionary preached in her kraal ?   Very seldom on a Sabbath evening did he find her sober, and he recalls that his last meeting with her, before she appeared in church, was indeed depressing.   He came away with the feeling that it might be as profitable to speak on soul matters to an ox as to her.   Yet on the first day on which she came to church she stayed behind the others, and asked the Missionary and the Elder to pray for her.   But let us hear the story in her own words.   " Some time back a burden began to come on me.   At first I did not know what it was, but in time it became quite distinct to my mind—it was my sins.   The more I tried to put it away the heavier it grew, and I lost all interest in life ; beer itself lost its taste and I grew more and more troubled.   The thing that puzzled me most was the question : ' Where did this burden come from ? Who was laying it on me ? ' I knew nothing of God and did not connect the placing of the burden with Him, although I knew that He was angry with sinners.   In this state I kept silent for a long time, but it would not do—I had to speak.   One day I mentioned the matter to one of your women members, and she at once said, ' Your burden is your sins ; God has put it on you, and try as you may you cannot get rid of it unless you go to church to hear the preaching.'   I went to church, but for a time the burden grew heavier.   However, I believed what the woman said and kept going, and sure enough one day as the preacher told of the Son of God bearing the sins of his people, it came as a flash to me that He was there on the Cross bearing away mine also.   I went home a happy woman—my burden all taken away by Jesus."   " Do you ever feel a burden of sin now ?"   " Yes, a little burden, a daily burden ; but it is not heavy as before."   " Why do you call it a *little* burden ?"   " Well, before, I could see no way of getting rid of it, but now it is little because I have been taught what to do with it when I feel it. I just go to Jesus with it and wait until I see Him again on the Cross taking it away.   *That always gives me peace.*"   (" The wayfaring men, though fools, shall not err therein.")

Now take Malota.   On our first meeting with her a number of years ago, we were introduced to her as one of King Lobengula's wives and grandmother of Esther, a girl member we were interested

in.   Tall, of commanding appearance, intelligent
looking, yet every inch a heathen ; a drinker, given
to fighting and filthy language, she was bound to be
a power on whatever side she should be found. Last
June she came before the Session and all were satisfied that a real change had come over her.   She
could give a good account of the power of the
Word, too.   But there was one thing Malota
would not do—she would not give up drinking a
little beer with her old friends as they met together
to speak.   She insisted that, since she was converted this habit did not rightly debar her from
membership.   Very gently she was told that what
she said was in part true, but that there was a law
in the Bible which made it sinful to be a stumbling
block to others ; that her example might lead others
to think lightly of the sin of drunkenness.   But
nothing could persuade her of this.   We asked her
if the Lord would give her light, and if He showed
her that it was wrong, would she give it up then ?
To this she replies.   " Yes."   " Well, this is the
way for you to take ; go and ask the Lord about it in
prayer and come back next quarter."   She came
back and was simply asked what answer had she
from the Lord.   Up she rose to her full height,
fists clenched, arms outstretched.   " Answer, yes
there is an answer, He showed me that it is altogether wrong ; I am finished with beer altogether."
This with all the force at her command.   " Where-
fore, if meat make my brother to offend, I will
eat no flesh while the world standeth, lest I make my
brother to offend."

(Malota died some years later at a great age, and to the end she remained faithful. Her last words were: " Receive Thou me O Lord of Glory.")

SPEAK THE TRUTH

When you've been guilty of a fault,
    Oh, lie not to conceal it,
For it will happen soon or late
    That something will reveal it.

And then, whate'er the deed has been,
    However great your trouble,
The faults, the sorrows, and the sin,
    Will all be rendered double.

But when at once the truth you've told,
    Away with all your sadness:
The sense of having done what's right
    Will fill your heart with gladness.

WILLIAM SALISBURY: A STORY FOR THE YOUNG

A person who was in Wiltshire about the latter end of the year 1813, heard a pleasing account of a little boy, who had recently died at a village near Trowbridge.   Not meeting with any one who could vouch for its authenticity, it is only very lately, on endeavouring to procure suitable tracts for very young persons, that the recollection of the circumstances induced an inquiry to be made of the minister of the place.   The reply appears so interesting, that it ought not to be buried in silence ; so encouraging to penitent sinners, that it should not be withheld from them ; and so great a call to the thoughtless and obdurate, that it is a duty to offer it to them.   It is as follows :—Respected, though unknown friend.   This morning I received your letter, respecting the dear little boy, who died in this village some time in the month of May, 1813.   The whole of the account you have sent in yours, is correct, except that the mother of the late child was not a widow, but was living with her husband at the time the boy died.   The woman and her husband were notoriously wicked, they paid no regard to the Sabbath, and every species of wickedness was committed with impunity.   The woman had the poor boy in question, before she was married to her present husband ; and they were also in very abject circumstances at the time the boy died.   Although I had been constantly preaching in the village for nearly seven years, I never saw either of them at the meeting in my life.   Indeed I did not know there were such people in the parish.

I relate all this, in order that you may have a clear understanding of the circumstances: the sequel of which will, I believe, be considered by you, a grand display of the free and rich grace and mercy of our good and gracious God, towards the vilest returning sinners.   And, as I find you are disposed to publish this affair, I feel it my duty to give you the full statement of it, as it came under my own cognizance, being nearly concerned.   I hope I feel thankful in my heart that you are stirred up to this: and may the Lord bless you in the work, and make it abundantly useful.   As near as I can recollect, the matter was as follows:—One evening, some friends being at my house, in Christian conversation, a person knocked at the door.   Opening it myself, I saw a tall bold-looking woman, in very mean attire.   Upon inquiring what she wanted, she told me, she came to ask me to go with her, to see her boy, who had been ill some little time, and she believed would not live the night over; and he had been begging them to send for Mr Dymott.   At length she was obliged to come, for the boy would not be quiet, he wanted so much to see Mr Dymott. I replied, " I do not know you, where do you live?" She answered, " About half a mile off."   " Why," said I, " I never saw you at our place of worship." " No Sir," said she, " I never go anywhere on a ' Sunday,' I have no clothes fit to go out in."   Said I to her, " How does your boy know me?" " Why," she said, " he has been in the habit of going to your meeting, whenever he could get away unobserved by me; for I did not let him every time he wanted to go, because he was so ragged, and had no shoes to wear; so that I was ashamed for him to go." She seemed much affected when relating this. She proceeded to say, that when he could get off to a meeting on a Sabbath day, he would be talking about the text and the sermon, nearly all the week after (but you shall hear more of this in its proper place). Requesting one of my friends to accompany me, we set off about nine o'clock the same evening: when we got to the house, I heard him talk to the people with him, before I got upstairs. Upon some one saying as I entered the room, " Here is Mr Dymott," the poor child looked up, put out his hand, and taking mine in his, thus addressed me: " Oh! Mr Dymott why had you not come before to me?" I replied, " I do not know anything of you nor of your wanting to see me." " Ah no," he replied, " I could not get my mother to come for you. But I am going to die, I am going to heaven, I am going to have a crown of life, and there is one prepared for you, and you and I shall be in heaven together. O! my dear Jesus, I want to come to heaven to you, I want to die this night." As he addressed me by name, I asked him how he knew me. " O," said he, " by going to hear you preach." Upon asking him when he went, he replied " Every time I could, when my mother would let me." I then enquired if he could remember anything he had heard me preach about. He answered, " Yes, that I can, I

heard you preach from that text, ' Let the wicked
forsake his way, and the unrighteous man his
thoughts, and let him return unto the LORD, and
He will have mercy upon him ; and to our God, for
he will abundantly pardon.'' This was repeated
correctly, though he could not read a word. All
this while, he appeared as happy as it was possible
for a creature to be, and at every interval in the
conversation, he would keep on saying, with great
earnestness, '' O my dear Jesus, I want to die, to
be out of this wicked world.'' This he would repeat twenty times following, with his hands and
eyes lifted to heaven, with as much propriety, grav-
ity, and seriousness as though he had been forty
years of age. I then asked him, if he would not be
glad to get better and have good clothes, so that he
might come to meeting on a Sabbath. '' O no,''
was the reply, '' I want to die and get out of this
wicked world.'' I think I shall never forget the
scene around me ; the room was full of people, and
everybody so affected, that all wept together. I
then availed myself of the opportunity of addressing those that never went to a place of worship on
the Lord's Day. Every now and then, the boy
would say, '' Hark ! Hark ! I hear music, music, I
hear music !'' whilst he pointed upwards with his
finger ; so that it really seemed as though a part
of heaven was let down into his soul, even while in
the body ; and when he could not hear the music,
he would say to his mother, '' I want to hear the
music again ;'' and then, '' Dear Jesus, I want to
come to heaven to you.'' Thus in the simplicity
and out of the fulness of his heart he spake. I

stayed an hour with him, and before I left, asked,
if I should attempt to pray with him.   " O yes."
After prayer, I took my leave, telling him I would
see him again in the morning.   Accordingly about
six o'clock the next day I went again ; but before I
got there, his prayer had been answered ; for he
died about three o'clock in the morning, and I was
informed, continued to the last in the same state I
saw him in.

When he was dead, his mother requested he
might be buried in our meeting-yard ; to which we
consented.

On the day of his burial I preached from the
words : " Jesus answered and said, I thank thee, O
Father, Lord of heaven and earth, because thou hast
hid these things from the wise and prudent, and
hast revealed them unto babes."   Astonishing to
relate, we had people from five to six miles around
us present at this time, and the concourse was so
great that it was supposed hundreds went away,
not being able to get near enough to the chapel to
hear.   This was the end of this dear child.   I
afterwards heard, from his mother and others, that
he would get away Sabbath mornings, and not go
back to get food, lest his mother should not permit
him to go again.   In this way he had stayed the
three services of the day, when the snow was on
the ground and he had no shoes to his feet and
loitered about from the end of one to the beginning
of the succeeding opportunity.   But had this been
known, he would not have fared thus.

I will now inform you a little what effect this had upon his then wicked mother.   She, seeing the happy end of her child, began to reflect upon her hard and cruel treatment of him ; which so wrought upon her mind, that she was like a distracted woman for many months, not capable of doing her labour. The Lord also gave her light to see her sin, as well as her ill usage of her child on account of his religion, the guilt of which so oppressed her, that she would lie down upon the ground and roll herself in agony, expecting every minute to be cut off and sent to destruction.   She began immediately to attend the means of grace, not only on the Lord's Day, but at our meetings of prayer.   Her wicked oaths and wicked companions and conduct were immediately left, and her cry was, " God be merciful to me a sinner."   She acknowledged to me, that she often cursed the boy ; for, after having been to meeting on a Sabbath, he would be talking to himself of what Mr Dymott said—often repeating these words :   " Let the wicked forsake his way," etc. when his mother would curse him, and say, " Mind your work, you lazy blockhead : what do you know about the wicked forsaking his way ?" and very often beat him into the bargain.   But after his death, this language to and usage of her child, and all upon account of his religion, recurred to her recollection, striking like daggers into her conscience ; and for a long season she went under great terrors of mind.   But at length the Lord was pleased to speak peace to her soul, after which she became a member of our society, and I believe her to be now a woman of sterling piety ; and though remarkably poor, yet she is an ornament to her profession ; and as she was notorious for wickedness, so now she seems to be eminent for rich and sound experience as a Christian ; and a more evident or extraordinary conversion I have never heard of.   Nor did the matter end here ; for, at the same time, this circumstance was blessed to the conversion of four or five of her wicked companions, who were reclaimed from the error of their ways.

> " God moves in a mysterious way,
>   His wonders to perform."

Thus I have given you as correct a statement of this affair as I am capable of, all which I was ear and eye-witness to.

The poor creature is now realizing great tribulation : her husband is lying ill in a dropsy, expecting him to die almost every day ; and were it not for the help of her friends, they must famish.   The parish officers will not allow them anything unless the poor man goes after it himself, and that is impossible for him to do in his present state ; but still the poor woman is in good spirits : she says she believes the Lord will provide somehow or other for her to get some food for her husband as long as he lives.

THE HAPPY MAN

By the Rev. Lachlan MacKenzie, Lochcarron

The happy man was born in the city of Regeneration in the parish of Repentance unto Life. He was educated at the school of Obedience. He has a large estate in the county of Christian Contentment, and many times does jobs of self-denial, wears the garment of Humility, and has another suit to put on when he goes to Court, called the Robe of Christ's Righteousness. He often walks in the valley of Self-Abasement, and sometimes climbs the mountains of Heavenly-mindedness. He breakfasts every morning on Spiritual Prayer, and sups every evening on the same. He has meat to eat that the world knows not of, and his drink is the sincere milk of the Word of God. Thus happy he lives, and happy he dies. Happy is he who has Gospel Submission in his will, due order in his affections, sound peace in his conscience, real divinity in his breast; the Redeemer's yoke on his neck, a vain world under his feet, and a crown of glory over his head. Happy is the life of that man who believes firmly, prays fervently, walks patiently, works abundantly, lives holily, dies daily, watches his heart, guides his senses, redeems his time, loves Christ, and longs for glory. He is necessitated to take the world on his way to heaven, but he walks through it as fast as he can, and all his business by the way is to make himself and others happy. Take him all in all, in two words, he is a Man and a Christian.

KITTY SMITH

Catharine Smith was a native of Pabay, a small island in Loch Roag, Skye, where dwelt seven families. From their insular situation and poverty, it had not been in the power of the parents to educate their children ; but little Kitty is an example of the truth that all God's children are taught of Him, for when only two years old she was observed to lay aside her playthings, and clasp her little hands with reverence during family worship ; and at the age of three she was in the habit of repeating the 23rd Psalm with such relish and fervour, as showed that she looked to the Good Shepherd in the character of a lamb of His flock. Her parents taught her also the Lord's Prayer, which she repeated duly, not only at her stated times, but often in the silence of night. She frequently pressed the duty of prayer, not only on the other children, but on her parents, and she told her father that, in their absence, when she would ask a blessing on the food left for the children, her brothers and sisters would mock at, and beat her for doing so. At another time, when she was probably about six years old, she was out with her companions herding cattle, when she spoke to them of the comeliness of Christ. They, probably to tempt her, said He was black. She left them, and returned home much cast down, and said : '' The children vexed me very much to-day. I will not go with them, for they said that Christ was black, and that grieved my spirit.'' Her parents asked her what she replied to that. '' I told them," she said, " that Christ is white and glorious in His apparel."

It is probable that Kitty was sufficiently enlightened to discern the moral comeliness of the gracious Redeemer, while her thoughtless comrades did not extend their ideas beyond personal beauty.   They would have said anything that might produce the effect of provoking their playfellow, whose more intelligent spirit grieved for them that they " saw no beauty in Him " whom her soul loved, " that they should desire Him." Perhaps no Christian character is truly confirmed in faith and patience, without some trial of persecution, which both shows to the heart its own corruption, by the irritating effects of gainsaying, and affords an opportunity of proving that we are not ashamed of the Gospel of Christ.   This dear child had her trial adapted to her age and sphere, and came forth on the Lord's side holding fast the word of life in as firm a way as a much more experienced Christian might have done.

The Rev. J. Macdonald, of Ferintosh, having preached in the parish of Uig, Skye, Kitty's parents were among the many who went to hear him.   On their return they mentioned what he had said about the formality of much that is called prayer, and the ignorance of many as to its spirituality ; they stated, according to their recollection of the sermon, that many had old, useless prayers, and greatly needed to learn to pray with the Spirit.   The child observed this, and two days after, said to her mother,

" It is time for me to give over my old form of prayer."   Her mother replied, " Neither you nor your prayers are old," but she replied, " I must give them over, and use the prayers which the Lord will teach me."   After this she withdrew to retired spots for prayer.   At one time her younger sister returned without her, and on being asked where she had left Kitty, she said, " I left her praying." Her father says that he has often sat up in bed listening to her sweet young voice, presenting this petition with heartfelt earnestness, " Oh, redeem me from spiritual and eternal death."

From the remoteness of her dwelling, Kitty had never attended any place of public worship— but the Sabbath was her delight—and often would she call in her brothers and sisters from the play in which they were thoughtlessly engaged, asking them to join in prayer and other devout exercises, and warning them, that if they profaned the day, and disliked God's worship, they must perish.   Her mother observing the intent gaze with which she looked on a large fire, enquired what she saw in the fire ?   She replied, " I am seeing that my state would be awful if I were to fall into that fire, even though I should be immediately taken out ; but woe is me, those who are cast into hell fire will never come out thence."   Another day, when walking by the side of a precipice, and looking down, she exclaimed to her mother, " How fearful would our state be if we were to fall down this rock, even though we should be lifted up again ; but they who are cast into the depths of hell will never be raised therefrom."

One day her mother found her lying on a bench with a sad countenance, and addressed some jocular words to her with a view to cheer her. But the child's heart was occupied with solemn thoughts of eternity; and instead of smiling, she answered gravely, " O, mother, you are vexing my spirit, I would rather hear you praying." In truth, eternity was very near her, and the Spirit of God was preparing her for entering it. As she got up one morning, she said, " O, are we not wicked creatures who have put Christ to death." Her mother, curious to hear what one so young could say on such a subject, replied, " Christ was put to death, Kitty, long before we were born." The child, speaking with an understanding heart, said, " Mother, I am younger than you, but my sins were crucifying Him." After a pause she added, " What a wonder that Christ could be put to death when He Himself was God, and had power to kill everyone; indeed, they only put Him to death as man, for it is impossible to kill God." She often used to repeat passages from Peter Grant's Spiritual Songs, such as " It is the blood of the Lamb that precious is." When she came to the conclusion of the verse, " It is not valued according to its worth," she would in touching terms, lament the sad truth, that His blood is so lightly thought of. Being present when some pious persons spoke of those in Rev. vii. who have washed their robes and made them white in the blood of the Lamb, she said, " Is it not wonderful that, while other blood stains what is dipped in it, this cleanses and makes white."

Murdoch Macleod being engaged in the valuable duties of a Scottish Elder in the tiny island of Pabay, Kitty wished much to hear him, but from bashfulness was ashamed to enter the house where he was employed in worship ; she therefore climbed up to the window and sat there till all was over.   Being asked what she had heard, she said she was amazed to hear that Christ offered Himself as a Saviour to many in our land who rejected Him, and that He was now going to other and more remote quarters to win souls.   She then added with the pathos of a full heart, " O, who knows but He may return here again."

Soon after she had completed her seventh year she was attacked by that sickness which opened her way to the Kingdom of Heaven.   When her father asked whom she pitied most of those she would leave behind, she replied that she pitied everyone whom she left in a Christless state.   She suffered much from thirst during her illness, and her mother, reluctant to give her so much cold water as she longed for, fell upon the evil expedient of telling her that the well was dried up.   The following day, when she saw water brought in for household purposes, poor Kitty's heart was grieved, and she said, " O, mother dear, was it not you who told the great lie yesterday, when you said the well was dry.

O, never do so again, for it angers God." During her illness, she was enabled almost literally to obey the command, "pray without ceasing," and was often interceding with the Lord to look down and visit her native place. On the morning of her last day on earth, her father said, "there is a reason for thankfulness that we see another day." Kitty opened her eyes, and said, "O Holy One of Israel, save me from death," a petition often used when in perfect health, and evidently referring to spiritual and eternal death. Throughout the day she was generally silent, when her father remarked, saying, "I do not hear you praying as usual;" to which she replied, "Dear father, I pray without ceasing, though not because you desire me to do so." In her last moments she was heard to say, "O, redeem me from death." Her father, leaning over her, said, "Kitty where are you now?" To which the reply was, "I am on the shore;" and immediately her soul was launched into the great ocean of eternity. In December 1829 this lowly child was carried from her poor native island to the blessed region where the redeemed of the Lord find their home, and her name has left a sweet perfume behind it.—"History of Revivals of Religion in the British Isles."

THE CONVERSION OF AFRICANER, THE NOTORIOUS SOUTH AFRICAN CHIEF

One of the most remarkable cases of conversion in modern times is that of the notorious African Chief Africaner. " His name," says the biographer of Robert Moffat, " carried dismay even to the solitary wastes." A Namaqua chief, pointing to Africaner, said to Robert Moffat :—" Look, there is the man, once the lion at whose roar even the inhabitants of distant hamlets fled from their homes. Yes, and I, for fear of his approach, fled with my people, our wives and children, to the mountain glen or to the wilderness, and spent nights among beasts of prey rather than gaze on the eyes of this lion, or hear his roar." He was the terror of the white and coloured races in Cape Colony, and the Government placed a considerable sum upon his head if so be that the country would be rid of this scourge and terror. But God can tame where man is helpless. Under the preaching of the Gospel by Mr Ebner, Africaner became as a lamb—the wild, roaring beast of prey became meek and subdued. When on a visit to Cape Town, Moffat purposed to take Africaner with him, but the chief at first refused, reminding the missionary that a sum of money had been placed on his head, and that the Government officers would hang him when he reached Cape Town. At length on receiving assurances of protection from Moffat, he

was willing to accompany him.   On the southward
journey Moffat called at a Boer farm, and on an-
nouncing to the farmer that he was Robert Moffat,
the missionary, he received the unexpected reply—
" Don't come near me, you have been long ago
murdered by Africaner."   " I am no ghost," pro-
tested Moffat.   The man was not reassured, and
only became more alarmed as he added—" Everybody says you were murdered, and a man told me
he had seen your bones."   Moffat assured him
that no such calamity had overtaken him, and that
Africaner was now a changed man, but on learning
that this man's uncle had been murdered by Africaner, he deemed it wise not to make known for
the present at least that the dreaded Africaner was
the man that accompanied him.   After a time,
however, he introduced the Boer to Africaner, and
the simple-minded, pious farmer lifted his two
hands to heaven and gave praise to the God of all
grace in these words :—" O Lord, what a miracle
of Thy power !   What cannot Thy grace accomplish !"

ARCHIBALD BOYLE: AN AUTHENTIC STORY

A hundred years ago there was in Glasgow a club of gentlemen of the first rank in that city. They met professedly for card-playing, but the members were distinguished by such a fearless excess of profligacy as to obtain for it the name of "The Hell Club." They gloried in the name they had acquired for themselves, and nothing that could merit it was left untried. Besides their nightly or weekly meetings, they held a grand annual festival, at which each member endeavoured to "outdo all his former outdoings" in drunkenness, blasphemy, and other sins. Of all who shone on these occasions none shone half so brilliantly as Archibald Boyle. He had been at one time a youth of the richest promise, being possessed of dazzling talents and fascinating manners. No acquirement was too high for his ability; but, unfortunately, there was none too low for his ambition! Educated by a fond and foolishly indulgent mother, he early met in society with members of "The Hell Club." Long ere he was five-and-twenty he was one of the most accomplished blackguards it could number on its lists. To him what were Heaven, Hell, or Eternity? Words, that served no purpose but to point his blasphemous wit or nerve his execrations. Alas! as soon as man forgets God, who alone can keep him, his understanding becomes darkened, and he glories in that which is his shame.

One night, on retiring to sleep, after returning from an annual festival of the club, Boyle dreamt that he was still riding, as usual, upon his famous black horse towards his own house—then a country seat embowered by ancient trees upon a hill—and that he was suddenly accosted by some one whose personal appearance he could not, in the gloom of night, distinctly discern, but who seizing the reins, said in a voice apparently accustomed to command, " You must go with me."   " And who are you ?" exclaimed Boyle, as he struggled to disengage his reins from the intruder's grasp. " That you will see by and by," replied the same voice in a cold sneering tone that thrilled through his very heart.   Boyle plunged his spurs into the panting sides of his steed.   The noble animal reared, and then suddenly darted forward with a speed that nearly deprived his rider of breath ; but in vain, in vain!—fleeter than the wind he flew, the mysterious, half-seen guide still before him ! Agonised by he knew not what, of indescribable horror and awe, Boyle again furiously spurred the gallant horse.   It fiercely reared and plunged, he lost his seat, and expected at the moment to feel himself dashed to the earth.   But not so, for he continued to fall—fall—fall—it appeared to himself, with an ever-increasing velocity.   At length this terrific rapidity of motion abated, and to his amazement and horror he perceived that his mysterious attendant was close by his side.   " Where ?" he exclaimed, in the frantic energy of despair, " where are you taking me ?   Where am I—where am I going ?"   " To Hell !" replied the same iron voice, and from the depths below the sound so familiar to his lips was suddenly re-echoed. " To Hell!" Onward, onward, they hurried in darkness, rendered more horrible still by the conscious presence of his spectral conductor. At length a glimmering light appeared in the distance, and soon increased to a blaze; but, as they approached it, in addition to the hideously discordant groans and yells of agony and despair, his ears were assailed with what seemed to be the echoes of frantic revelry. They soon reached an arched entrance of such stupendous magnificence that all the grandeur of this world seemed in comparison but as the frail and dingy labours of the poor mole. Within it, what a scene!—too awful to be described. Multitudes gnashing their teeth in the hopelessness of despair; while memory, recalling opportunities lost and mercies despised, presented to their fevered mental vision the scenes of their past lives.

Boyle at length perceived that he was surrounded by those whom he had known on earth, but were some time dead, each one of them betraying his agony at the bitter recollections of the vain pursuits that had engrossed his time here—time lent to prepare for a far different scene! Suddenly observing that his unearthly conductor had disappeared, he felt so relieved by his absence that he ventured to address his former friend, Mrs D——, whom he saw sitting with eyes fixed in intense earnestness, as she was wont on earth, apparently absorbed at her favourite game of loo. " Ha, Mrs D——! delighted to see you; d'ye know a

fellow told me to-night he was bringing me to Hell!
—ha, ha! If this be Hell," said he, scoffingly,
" what a precious pleasant place it must be!—ha,
ha! Come now, my good Mrs D——, for auld
lang syne do just stop for a moment's rest, and "
—" show me through the pleasures of Hell," he
was going, with reckless profanity, to add; but with
a shriek that seemed to pierce through his very
soul, she exclaimed, " Rest! there is no rest in
Hell!" and from interminable vaults, voices, as
loud as thunder, repeated the awful, the heart-
withering sound, " There is no rest in Hell!" And
they laughed for they had laughed on earth at all
that is good and holy. And they sang—profane
and blasphemous songs sang they, for they had
often done so on earth, at the very hour God claims
as His own—the still and mid-night hour. And
he who, in his vision, walked among them in a
mortal frame of flesh and blood, felt how inexpress-
ibly more horrible such sounds could be than ever
was the wildest shriek of agony on earth. And
this was Hell!—the scoffer's jest, the by-word of
the profligate.

All at once he perceived that his unearthly
conductor was once more by his side. " Take
me," shrieked Boyle, " take me from this place!
By the living God, whose Name I have so often out-
raged, I adjure thee, take me from this place!"
" Can'st thou still name His Name?" said the
fiend, with a hideous sneer. " Go, then; but—
in a year and a day we meet to part no more."
Boyle awoke, and he felt as if the last words of the

fiend were traced in letters of living fire upon his heart and brain. He resolved, utterly and for ever, to forsake " The Club." Above all, he determined that nothing on earth should tempt him to join the next annual festival. The companions of his licentiousness soon flocked around him, and finding that his deep dejection of mind did not disappear with his bodily ailment, and that it arose from some cause which disinclined him from seeking or enjoying their accustomed orgies, they became alarmed with the idea of losing " the life of the Club," and they bound themselves by an oath never to desist till they had discovered what was the matter with him, for one of their number declared, that on unexpectedly entering Boyle's room, he detected him in the act of hastily hiding a book, which he actually believed was the Bible.

After a time one of his compeers, more deeply cunning than the rest, bethought himself of assuming an air of the deepest disgust with the world, the Club, and the mode of life they had been pursuing. He affected to seek Boyle's company in a mood of congenial melancholy, and to sympathise in all his feelings. Thus he succeeded in betraying him into a much-misplaced confidence as to his dream, and the effect it had produced upon his mind. The result may be readily guessed. His confidence was betrayed, his feelings of repentance ridiculed, and it will easily be believed that he who " hid the Bible " had not nerve to stand the ribald jests of his profligate companions. From the annual meeting he shrunk with an instinctive horror, yet found

himself, he could not tell how, seated at that table
on that very day where he had sworn to himself
a thousand and a thousand times nothing on earth
should make him sit.   His ears tingled, and his
eyes swam, as he listened to the opening sentence
of the president's address : " Gentlemen, this is
leap year ; therefore it is a year and a day since our
last annual meeting."   Every nerve in Boyle's
body twanged in agony at the ominous, the well-
remembered words.   His first impluse was to rise
and flee ; but then—the sneers ! the sneers ! How
many in this world, as well as poor Boyle, have sold
their souls to the dread of a sneer, and dared the
wrath of an almighty and eternal God, rather than
encounter the sarcastic curl of a fellow-creature's
lip.

    The night was gloomy, with frequent and fitful
gusts of chill and howling wind, as Boyle, with
fevered nerves and a reeling brain, mounted his
horse to return home.   The following morning the
well-known black steed was found, with saddle and
bridle on, quietly grazing by the road-side, about
half-way to Boyle's country house, and a few yards
from it lay the stiffened corpse of its master !

    God, who has the power of communicating
with the minds of His creatures, did doubtless speak
by a dream to poor Archibald Boyle and through
the same dream He now speaks to you.   The
dream is horrible—truly horrible, yet not half so
horrible as the reality.   Ah, no ! no dream can
picture the full, long misery of " the worm that
dieth not," " the fire that is never quenched,"
the woe that never ends.   Had the poor dreamer

gone direct from his sense of Hell to Christ, to Him who died to save us from its coming wrath, how different his end!   In Christ he would have found a deliverer from Hell, for in Him he would have found One, who, sinless Himself, was competent to undertake the sinner's cause, and who had borne the dreadful judgment of sin in His own blessed Person.   And it is the belief of the Gospel which gives peace and power over sin.

Reader, let these words sound in your ears, but drink in also the glad tidings of salvation which proclaim to you that the judgment due to the sinner, Christ has suffered, for " He was wounded for our transgressions, He was bruised for our iniquities."   He died for the sinner—the vilest and the greatest—that the sinner believing in Jesus " should not perish, but have everlasting life " (John iii. 16).   Oh, accept even now the salvation of God ere it be too late!

> " O taste and see that God is good :
>   who trusts in him is bless'd.
> Fear God his saints : none that him fear
>   shall be with want oppress'd.
> The lions young may hungry be,
>   and they may lack their food :
> But they that truly seek the Lord
>   shall not lack any good.
> O children, hither do ye come,
>   and unto me give ear ;
> I shall you teach to understand
>   how ye the Lord should fear."
>   **Met. Psalm 34, v. 8—11**

LETTER TO A SOUL SEEKING JESUS

Taste that Christ is precious.

December, 1841.

DEAR FRIEND—It is written, " *Unto you there-fore which believe He is precious,*" and if you are a child of God you will know and feel what the words mean. I. Peter ii. 7. At one time Christ was as a tender plant " to you, and like " a root out of a dry ground." You saw no form nor comeliness in Him, no beauty that you should desire Him. At that time you were at ease in Zion—you had no concern for your soul. Do you remember that time? Is it otherwise with you now? Have you been pricked in your heart by the Holy Spirit? Have you been made to see how impossible it is for man to be just with God? and has the Spirit drawn away the veil from the fair face of Immanuel, and given you an unfeigned glance at the brow that was crowned with the thorns, and the cheek from which they plucked off the hair? Has the Spirit opened a window into the heart of Jesus, and let you see the fountain head of that love that " passeth knowledge?" Then you will be able to say, " To me *He is precious.*" If you see plainly that all your standing before God is in Him, that He is your foundation-stone—your fountain—your wedding garment, then you will feel Him to be pre-cious. Most people refuse to come to Christ. Read Luke xiv. 16—24. They all with one con-sent began to make excuse. Why is this? Just because they do not see and feel that He is precious.   But, oh! if you, my dear friend, feel that He is your only righteousness—your only fountain of living water—your high priest—your shepherd —your advocate ; then you will say, " *He is precious*!"   You will never say, " Have me excused." I carry to you the sweet invitation, " Come, for all things are now ready."   Jesus is ready to wash and clothe you in his own blood and righteousness. The Holy Spirit is ready to come into your heart and make it new.   The Father is ready to put his arms round your neck and kiss you.   Luke xv. 20.   The angels are ready to give thanks for you and to love you as a sister for eternity.   Now, will you come, for *all things are ready?*   Are you now saying in your heart, " I cannot but believe I am the chief of sinners, and Jesus offers to be my refuge, my mediator, my all in all ; I feel He is precious ?"   O dear friend, I trust you do.   This only will make you happy in living, and blessed in dying.   This is a poor dying world.   Man that is born of a woman is of few days and full of trouble. There is no part here that death cannot take from us.   But if you have Christ, you have the only imperishable portion!   Oh, may the Holy Spirit give you a firm hold of Jesus.   Then we shall meet in that sweet place, where there shall be no more death, neither sorrow nor crying, neither shall there be any more pain.   The Lord deal kindly and gently with you, both soul and body.   Farewell, dear friend.   Ever yours,

Robt. Murray McCheyne.

LUTHER AND THE COUNT

In the year 1518, on the evening of the 8th April, Count Eberhard might be seen as he galloped over the bridge of his castle at Erbach, so fast that his followers could hardly keep up with him.   It had cost him a hard struggle to leave home at this time, for in one of the chambers his little daughter, Hildegard, was lying to all appearance at the point of death.   The Countess strove lo detain him, but it was all to no purpose ; his determination was fixed ; he tore himself away, though a severe pang pierced his heart as he bade his wife farewell and cast a last look on his child's pale form.   In the autumn of the preceding year, God had caused the long-forgotten word of His grace in His Son Christ Jesus to be once more proclaimed at Wittenberg by His servant, Martin Luther, and within a fortnight it had spread through almost all parts of Germany, and found an entrance into many hearts.   But, as always happens under such circumstances, it was attended with gainsaying and misunderstandings. While it met with acceptance among the common people, and even with many of the higher classes, who, amidst their outward splendour, had not hearts alive to their spiritual wants ; yet among the great and wise of this world there were those who attempted to '' kick against the pricks.''   To this latter class belonged Count Eberhard.   He threatened apostates from the Romish Church with the severest punishments, and roused the clergy of all ranks and orders to oppose the progress of heresy.   John Speckel, a man of learning, earnestly seconded his efforts ; but all attempts to shut out the new doctrine from the Count's domains were as powerless as if he had tried to stay the blasts that rushed through the valleys of the Odenwald.

The Count and his ecclesiastical fellow-workers were delighted when Eckius, Prierias and others took the field against Luther, but persons who were more far-sighted, and had read their writings, were disposed to believe that his cause would only be advanced by such opponents. Under all these attacks, Luther's own courage and faith waxed stronger ; and this year, on the 26th of April, when a meeting of the Augustin friars was to be held at Heidelberg, the undaunted Reformer, having provided himself with letters of introduction to the Prince Palatine, set out on foot.   He preached everywhere powerfully and humbly, giving all glory to the Lord.   From every quarter people flocked to see the man whose name had found its way into the most distant peasant's cottage.   No one was more indignant at Luther's popularity than Count Eberhard.   At last his resolution was taken ; he would find it no difficult matter to attack the Reformer unawares, and might give him in custody to the monks till he consented to recant.

Count Eberhard felt satisfied and passed through the gate of Miltenberg.   The whole town was alive.   Groups of men were moving about the streets, and talking of the wonderful man to whose wonderful preaching they had been listening that day.   The Count dashed through the crowd

straight up to the inn near to which Luther had
taken up his quarters.   " My Lord Count," exclaimed the innkeeper, " I should never have
dreamt that Luther would have made your grace
stir from home !"   The Count made no reply and
withdrew at once to his bed-chamber.   Wearied
out by his hasty ride and mental agitation, he threw
himself on his bed, and dropped into a deep sleep.
After some hours he awoke, and as he wished to
keep awake, rose up, and went to the window.
Darkness and silence were spread over the little
town with its slumbering population.   The Count
was quite at a loss what course to take.

All of a sudden a light shone in the corner
chamber of the next house, and a deep, fine, manly
voice, which, in the silence of the night, fell on the
Count's ears quite audibly, uttered the words :
" This may God grant, the Father, Son, and Holy
Ghost.   Amen !" As the Count occupied the high-
est storey, he overlooked the chamber and he could
plainly discern the dark form of some one kneel-
ing down in prayer.   For a while this person
seemed to be turning over the leaves of a book,
and then began his prayer again : " Lord my God,
in Thee do I put my trust ; save me from all them
that persecute me, and deliver me ; lest they tear
my soul like a lion, while there is none to deliver."
these words were taken from Psalm vii.   The
Count had never before heard any one pray in this
manner ; each word in the lips of the worshipper
seemed like a sledge-hammer knocking at Heaven's
gate, especially the concluding verses : " My de-

fence is of God, which saveth the upright in heart.
God judgeth the righteous, and is angry with the
wicked every day.   If he turn not, He will whet His
sword, He hath bent His bow, and made it ready.''
These words were uttered with such power and
confidence that the Count could not help thinking :
'' Truly this man has a better shield than I have,
and a sharper sword.   With such a man I would
not wish to be otherwise than on good terms.''   And
when the person went on to pray for all Christen-
dom, that God would cause the clear light of the
Gospel to shine forth ; that He would turn the hearts
of princes as the rivers of water are turned, and
make the poor common people free by His truth,
and that as to the enemies of the Word, He would
crush their pride ; and that ignorant persecutors
might take warning by His judgments, and attend
to the one thing needful ; at the close of these peti-
tions the Count could not help clasping his hands,
and with tears in his eyes, he exclaimed aloud :
'' Amen ! Amen !   Grant it may be, O God, as
Thy servant has said.''

The Count walked up and down his chamber
restlessly occupied with the single thought of seeing
the man face to face whom he had heard praying
in this manner.   At last he noticed that the day
had begun.   He rang for the innkeeper, who immediately made his appearance with a tankard of
warm ale on a silver waiter which he was going to
place on the marble table.   But the Count stopped
him, saying :   '' Cannot you tell me who that person
is in yonder chamber with the curtain let down.''

" Certainly! And have you really seen him? Why, it is Luther the Arch-heretic. His lamp has been burning for some hours."

The Count stood thunder-struck. " Luther is it?" " Yes, Dr Martin Luther," said the inn-keeper, seeing his astonishment. " Has your Grace any commands to give?" but, receiving no answer, he made his bow and withdrew.

For some time the Count stood as if fixed to the spot. At last, without touching his break-fast, he hurried down stairs, went over to the next house, and stood in an instant before Luther. On the Count's entering, Luther rose from his seat, and beheld a portly figure in complete armour, and with his sword by his side, standing before him with an anxious look, but not uttering a word. But when at last in a kindly tone, Luther broke the silence by asking what he wanted, the Count fell on his knees, and exclaimed: " O Man! you are better than I am. God forgive me that I ever thought of doing you harm!" He then told what was his design in coming thither, and how he heard him pray, and how his words overpowered him.

" Not my word," said Luther, " but the Word of the Lord, which I, a poor unworthy sin-ner, have the honour of bringing into Germany. Go your way in peace, my Lord Count; He who has begun a good work in you will carry it on to the day of Jesus Christ. If it please God, you shall see still greater wonders, for ' He breaketh the bow and cutteth the spear in sunder.' His word they cannot destroy, for the Word of the Lord endureth for ever.''

The Count's attendants were waiting at the entrance of the inn, where they had been joined by Echter and Bernhold, expecting to receive his orders.   But he galloped passed them, and waving his hand, as if lost in thought, said : '' Go in peace ; the Word of the Lord endureth for ever.''   As he entered the gate way of the castle his wife came out to meet him and said their child had passed a good night and was sitting up in bed waiting for her father.

Without going into particulars, we may state that from that time the Count zealously endeavoured that the Word which he had persecuted might be published with all fidelity to his subjects. Among the Princes who were present at the Diet of Worms is to be found the name of Count Eberhard Von Erbach, as an enlightened friend of the Protestant cause, who there made a good confession on its behalf.

John Speckel also, formerly priest at Michelstadt, was the first of a succession of ministers who published the Gospel at Brensbach ; and on his pulpit, which was erected by Count Eberhard in the year 1526, is to be seen an inscription, which was then the watchword of Protestants :—'' The Word of the Lord endureth for ever.''

THE DUMB BOY'S EXAMINATION

A clergyman once paid a visit to a deaf and dumb asylum in London, for the express purpose of examining the children in the knowledge they possessed of divine truth.   A little boy, on this occasion, was asked in writing : " Who made the world ?"   He took up the chalk, and wrote underneath the question : " In the beginning God created the heaven and the earth."   The clergyman then inquired in a similar manner : " Why did Jesus Christ come into the world ?"   The little fellow wrote : " This is a faithful saying, and worthy of all acceptation, that Jesus Christ came into the world to save sinners."   A third question was then proposed, eminently adapted to call his most powerful feeling into exercise : " Why were you born deaf and dumb, while I can hear and speak ?" " Never," said an eye-witness, " shall I forget the look of holy resignation and chastened sorrow which sat on his countenance as he took up the chalk and wrote : ' Even so, Father, for so it seemed good in thy sight.' "

THE REV. TIMOTHY ROGERS AND HIS YOUTHFUL DEFENDER

Sir Richard Craddock, a justice of peace, who was a violent hater and persecutor of the Dissenters, and who exerted himself to enforce all the severe laws then in existence against them, happened to live near Mr Timothy Rogers, to whom he bore particular enmity, and whom he wanted above all things to have in his power.   Hearing that he was to preach at a place some miles distant, he thought it a fair opportunity for accomplishing his base design ; and in order thereto, hired two men to go as spies, and to take down the names of all the hearers whom they knew, that they might appear as witnesses against both them and Mr Rogers.   The plan seemed to succeed to his wishes.   These men brought him the names of several persons who were present at the meeting, and he warned such of them as he had a particular spite against, together with Mr Rogers, to appear before him.   Knowing the violence of the man, they came with trembling hearts, expecting to be treated with the utmost severity.   While they were waiting in the great hall, expecting to be called upon, a little girl, about six or seven years of age, who was Sir Richard's grand-daughter, happened to come into the hall. She looked at Mr Rogers, and was much taken with his venerable appearance.   He being naturally fond of children, took her upon his knee and caressed her, which occasioned her to conceive a great fondness for him.   At length Sir Richard sent a servant to inform them, that one of the witnesses being taken ill, was unable to attend, and that, therefore, they must come again another day. They accordingly came at the time appointed, and being convicted, the justice ordered their mittimus to be written to send them all to prison.

Mr Rogers expecting to see the little girl again, brought some sweetmeats with him to give her. As soon as she saw him she came running to him, and appeared fonder of him than before. This child being a particular favourite of her grandfather, had got such an ascendency over him that he could deny her nothing; and she possessed such a violent spirit that she could bear no contradiction, so that she was indulged in everything she wanted. At one time, when she had been contradicted, she ran a pen-knife into her arm, to the great danger of her life. This bad spirit, in the present instance, was over-ruled for good. While she was sitting on Mr Rogers' knee, eating the sweetmeats, she looked earnestly at him, and asked, " What are you here for, sir?" He answered, " I believe your grandfather is going to send me and my friends to jail." " To jail!" says she; " why, what have you done?" " Why, I did nothing but preach, and they did nothing but hear me." " He shall not send you to jail," replied she. " Ay, but my dear," said he, " I believe he is now making out our mittimus to send us all there." Upon this she ran up to the chamber where Sir Richard was, and knocked with her head and heels till she got in, and said to him, " What are you going to do with my good old gentleman in the hall ?'' '' That's nothing to you,'' said he; '' get about your business.'' '' But I won't,'' says she; '' he tells me that you are going to send him and his friends to jail; and if you send them, I'll drown myself in the pond as soon as they are gone; I will indeed.'' When he saw the child thus peremptory, it shook his resolution, and induced him to abandon his malicious design. Taking the mittimus in his hand, he went down into the hall, and thus addressed these good men :—'' I had here made out your mittimus to send you all to jail, as you deserve, but at my grandchild's request, I drop the prosecution, and set you all at liberty.'' They all bowed and thanked his worship. But Mr Rogers, going to the child, laid his hand upon her head, and lifting up his eyes to heaven, said, '' God bless you, my dear child! May the blessing of that God whose cause you did now plead, though as yet you know Him not, be upon you in life, at death, and to all eternity !'' He and his friends then went away.

The above remarkable story was told by Mr T. Rogers, the son of the ejected minister, who had frequently heard his father relate it with great pleasure; and the celebrated Mr Thomas Bradbury once heard it from him, when he was dining at the house of Mrs Tooley, an eminent Christian lady in London, who was distinguished for her religion, and for her love to Christ and His people; whose house and table, like Lydia's were always open to them.

What follows is yet more remarkable, as containing a striking proof of the answer which was returned to good Mr Rogers' prayers for this child, and the blessing which descended upon her who had been the instrument of such a deliverance for these persecuted servants of God.   Mrs Tooley had listened with uncommon attention to Mr Rogers' story; and when he had ended it, she asked him, '' And are you that Mr Rogers' son?''   He told her he was.   Upon which she said, '' Well, as long as I have been acquainted with you, I never knew that before.   And now I will tell you something which you do not know; I am the very girl your dear father blessed in the manner you have related, and it made an impression upon me which I could never forget.''   Upon this double discovery, Mr Rogers and Mrs Tooley found an additional tie of mutual love and affection; and then he and Mr Bradbury expressed a desire to know how she, who had been brought up in an aversion to the Dissenters, and to serious religion, now discovered such an attachment to both, upon which she cheerfully gave them the following narrative :—

After her grandfather's death she became sole heiress to his estate, which was considerable.   Being in the bloom of youth, and having none to control her, she ran into all the fashionable diversions of the age without any restraint.   But she confessed, that when the pleasurable scenes were over, she found a dissatisfaction, both with them and herself, that always struck a damp to her heart, which she did not know how to get rid of any other way than by running the same round over and over again; but all was in vain.   Having contracted

some slight illness, she thought she would go to
Bath, hearing that it was a place for pleasure as
well as health.   When she came thither, she was
providentially led to consult an apothecary who was
a very worthy and religious man.   When he inquired what ailed her, she answered, '' Why,
doctor, I don't ail much as to my body, but I have
an uneasy mind that I cannot get rid of.''   '' Truly, miss,'' said he, '' I was so till I met with a certain book, and that cured me.''   '' Books !'' said
she, '' I get all the books I can lay my hands on ;
all the plays, novels, and romances I hear of ; but
after I have read them my uneasiness is the same.''
'' That may be, miss,'' said he, '' and I do not
wonder at it.   But as to this book I speak of, I
can say of it what I can say of no other I ever read,
that I never tire in reading it, but can read it again,
as if I had never read it before, and I always see
something new in it.''   '' Pray, doctor,'' says she,
'' what book it that,''   '' Nay, miss,'' answered
he, '' that is a secret I don't tell everyone.'' '' But
could not I get a sight of that book ?'' says she.
'' Yes,'' replied he, '' if you speak me fair, I can
help you to a sight of it.''   '' Pray, then, get it
me, doctor, and I'll give you anything you please.''
'' Yes,'' said he, '' if you will promise me one thing,
I'll bring it you ; and that is, that you will read it
over carefully ; and if you should not see much in it
at first, that you will give it a second reading.''
She promised faithfully that she would.   After
coming two or three times without it, to raise her

curiosity, he at last took it out of his pocket, and gave it her.

This book was the New Testament.   When she looked at it, she said, with a flirt, " Pooh ! I could get that at any time."   " Why, miss," said he, " so you might ; but, remember, I have your solemn promise that you will read it carefully." " Well," says she, " though I never read it before, I'll give it a reading."   Accordingly she began to read it, and it soon attracted her attention.   She saw something in it wherein she had a deep concern ; but her mind now became ten times more uneasy than ever.   Not knowing what to do, she soon returned to London, resolved to try again what the diversions there would do to dissipate her gloom.   But nothing of this kind answered her purpose.   She lodged at the Court end of the town, where she had with her a female companion. One Saturday evening she had a remarkable dream, which was, that she was in a place of worship, where she heard a sermon ; but when she awoke she could remember nothing but the text.   This dream, however, made a deep impression upon her mind ; and the idea she had of the place, and of the minister's person, was as strong as if she had been long acquainted with both.   On the Lord's day morning she told her dream to her companion, and said, that after breakfast she was resolved to go in quest of the place, though she should go from one end of London to the other.   They accordingly set out, and went into several churches as they passed along, but none of them answered to what she saw in her dream.   About one o'clock they found themselves in the heart of the city, where they dined, and then set out again in search of this place of worship.

Being in the Poultry about half-an-hour after two o'clock, they saw a great number of people going down the Old Jewry, and she determined to see where they went.   She mingled with the company and they conducted her to the meeting-house in the Old Jewry, where Mr Shower was then minister.   As soon as she entered the door, and surveyed the place, she turned to her companion and said, with some surprise, " This is the very place I saw in my dream."   She had not been long there before she saw Mr Shower go up into the pulpit, and looking at him with greater surprise, she said, " This is the very man I saw in my dream ; and if every part of it hold true, he will take for his text, Ps. cxvi, 7, " Return unto thy rest, O my soul ; for the LORD hath dealt bountifully with thee."   When he rose up to pray, she was all attention, and every sentence went to her heart. Having finished his prayer, he took that very passage which she had mentioned for his text ; and God was pleased to make the discourse founded upon it the means of her saving conversion ; and thus she at last found what she had so long sought elsewhere in vain—rest to her soul.   And now she obtained that blessing from God, the Fountain of felicity, which godly Mr Rogers, so many years before, had so solemnly and fervently implored on her behalf.

THE HIGHLAND KITCHEN-MAID

There is scarcely a single district nowadays—Highland, Lowland, populous, desert, or beautiful—through which we cannot find a cheap and speedy means of transit.　It was not so, however, in the days of good old Hector McPhail, still the unforgotten pastor of Resolis.　Stage-coaches, canal-boats, steamers, and railways were alike unthought of in those latitudes and times, so that, however long and tedious the journey, however desolate and dangerous the roads, in the still comparatively lawless state of the Highland district, Mr McPhail's only resource was his shaggy little white steed, the close companion of his apostolic wanderings.　Oh, that faithful bearer of the remarkable man of God, what a wonderous biography it must have had ! How many a weary mile had it cheerfully trudged on its master's almost endless message of mercy and love ! Where is the moor or mountain of its native Ross of which the solitudes, however lonely, have not been trodden by its trusty feet ?　Even the bleak Slochdmuic, from whose dark and frowning precipices the eye of my own childhood turned shudderingly away as I asked of her who sat beside me, " Is this the old world, mamma ?" Even it, though buried deep in the gloomy glens of Badenoch, had echoed to the patter of its weary tread.　To how many a fervent prayer, unheard by human ear, has it been called to listen !　How many a dialogue, to be remembered throughout eternity, has its sagacity occasioned between its devoted master and a fellow sinner !　How many are the hours of searching self-examination, or silent study, or blessed communion with its master's God, that had been spent upon its back! Where was the shepherd or cottar that knew it not, as he saw by the moonbeam's light its white form move across the moor? And how many a night has its weather-beaten rider been forced to throw the reins upon its neck and to screen himself with his well-worn cloak against the pitiless fury of the storm, while neither pelting sleet nor drifting snow could blind the sharp eyes of his little steed, nor hinder it from bearing its sainted burden to the door of his moorland home!

Our story, however, dates far on in the month of May, a few days before the meeting of the General Assembly of the Scottish Establishment, to which Mr McPhail was proceeding as a commissioner from the Presbytery of Chanonry. Travelling at the rate of from thirty to forty miles a day, his journey would occupy a full week, and would frequently oblige him to pass the night in the then by no means comfortable inns upon the Highland road. It was Mr McPhail's invariable practice to hold family worship in these houses, and to insist upon the attendance of every individual inmate. Resting one night at a little inn amid the wild hills of Inverness-shire, he summoned, as usual, the family together for devotional purposes. When all had been seated, the Bibles produced, and the group awaiting the commencement of the devotions, Mr McPhail looked around him and asked whether every inmate of the house was present. The landlord replied in the affirmative.

" All?" again inquired the minister.

" Yes," answered the host, " we are all here; there is a little lassie in the kitchen, but we never think of asking her in, for she is so dirty that she is not fit to be seen."

" Then call in the lassie," said Mr McPhail, laying down the Bible which he had opened; " we will wait till she comes."

The landlord apologised. The minister was peremptory. " The scullery-maid had a soul, and a very precious one," he said, " if she was not in the habit of being summoned to family worship, all the greater was her need to joining them now." Not one word would he utter until she came. The host at length consented; the kitchen girl was taken in to join the circle, and the evening worship proceeded.

After the devotions were concluded, Mr McPhail called the little girl aside, and began to question her about her soul and its eternal interest. He found her in a state of the most deplorable ignorance.

" Who made you?" asked the minister, putting the usual introductory question to a child. The girl did not know.

" Do you know that you have a soul?"— " No; I never heard that I had one. What is a soul?"

" Do you ever pray?"—" I don't know what you mean."

" Well, I am going to Edinburgh, and I will bring you a little neckerchief if you promise to say a prayer that I will teach you; it is very short; there are only four words in it, ' Lord, show me myself '; and if you repeat this night and morning I will not forget to bring you what I have promised.''

The little kitchen-maid was delighted, a new piece of dress was a phenomenon she had rarely witnessed. The idea was enchanting; the condition was easy; the promise was given with all the energy of young expectancy; and Mr McPhail, after explaining, no doubt, the meaning and force of the prayer, retired to rest, and next morning resumed his journey.

Everyone must be aware that the visit of a Ross-shire minister to the metropolis is a sort of triennial era, even in these days of easy transport. Call this, and commission that, have to be executed; and if one be known to possess the least degree of the obliging in his character he has his hands full. Nevertheless, Mr McPhail did not forget the Highland inn and its little menial; but, relying upon the fulfilment of her promise, purchased the trifling present that was to make her happy.

Again, then, we accompany the devoted minister to the wild mountains of Badenoch, and at the close of a mild June evening reach the lonely Highland inn. The white pony is safely housed, and the minister, ere he permits supper to touch his lips, summons the household to the worship of God. Again, however, the little kitchen-maid is absent, and again he inquires the cause. But it is now a different reason that withholds her.

'' Indeed, sir,'' replied the hostess to Mr Mc-

Phail's inquiry, " she has been of little use since you were here; she has done nothing but sit and cry night and day, and now she is so weak and exhausted that she cannot rise from her bed."

" Oh, my good woman, let me see the poor girl immediately!" exclaimed the minister, instantly divining the reason of her grief.

He was conducted to a hole beneath the stairs where the little creature lay upon a straw bed, a picture of mental agony and spiritual distress.

" Well, my child," said the amiable man, affectionately addressing her, " here is the neckerchief I have brought you from Edinburgh; I hope you have done what you promised, and said the prayer that I taught you."

" Oh, no, sir, no, I can never take your present; a dear gift it has been to me; you taught me a prayer that God has answered in an awful way; He has shown me myself, and, oh, what a sight that is! Minister, Minister, what shall I do?"

I need not say how rejoiced the faithful man of God was to see that the Spirit of Jehovah had been dealing with this young soul, and that, although still operating as a " Spirit of bondage " in the production of a true though partial and imperfect faith, there were yet such hopeful signs that ere long He would exhibit Himself as the " Spirit of adoption," generating in her heart a full and perfect trust, and leading her to cry, " Abba, Father." But how reconcile such an experience with the strange opinion which denies to the Holy Ghost any special agency in conversion, giving to each of the

human race a certain amount of influence to be communicated only through the medium of the Word. Whence had this child derived, in the course of little more than a fortnight, and through the use of such a prayer, this experimental acquaintance with her own heart? Read the Word she could not; sympathy of feeling in the careless household was out of the question; whence, then, that mysterious ray which all at once illuminated the darkened chamber of the soul, and, as it shot its clear, strong light through the once benighted understanding, exposed in all its barrenness the deformity of self? It was the Spirit of God that wrought independently of the Word, and coming into " warm contact " with her living soul in a manner altogether special and hitherto unknown by herself or a carnal world. It was the " Spirit of Truth, whom the world cannot receive, because it seeth Him not, neither knoweth Him "; but she knew Him, for He dwelt with her, and was with her, and was in her. On no other principle can we account for the fact that one, but a few weeks ago so totally ignorant that she had asked, " What is a soul?" should now have been able to pursue that most difficult and severe of all subjective mental processes—the reflex inspection of self. Now, this is no fictitious case got up for the occasion; " I tell but what is told to me "; but who that reads it can deny the absolute necessity of a special agency and a personal and immediate indwelling of the blessed Spirit sent forth into the soul in answer to the prayer, " Lord, show me myself!"

After some further conversation, Mr McPhail opened up to the distressed girl the great Gospel method of salvation, and closed the interview by recommending the use of another and equally short and comprehensive prayer : " Lord, show me Thyself !"   Next morning the minister was once again on his way to his still distant home.   But he had " cast his bread upon the waters."   Did he ever " find it after many days ?"

Many years had passed since this memorable journey, and the vigorous and wiry minister who could ride forty miles a day for a week without intermission was now become an old and feeble man, worn out in the Master's service, scarcely any longer " spending," because already " spent " for Christ.   One day his servant intimated that a stranger was desirous to speak with him.   Permission being given, a respectable matronly woman was ushered into the study, carrying a large parcel in her hand.

" You will scarcely know me, Mr McPhail," said the person, with a modest and deferential air. The minister replied that he certainly did not recognise her.

" Do you remember a little scullery-maid at ————— inn, in whose soul you once took a deep interest, upon your journey to Edinburgh ?" Mr McPhail had a perfect recollection of the events.

" I was that little girl.   You taught me two short but most expressive prayers.   By the first I was brought to feel my need of a Saviour ; by the second I was led to behold that Saviour Himself

and to view Jehovah in the character of a reconciled
God and Father in Christ.   I am now respectably
married and comfortably settled in life, and although the mother of a numerous family, have
travelled far to see your face and to cheer you by
telling with my own lips the glorious things which,
by your means, the Lord has been pleased to do
for my soul.''

Before parting with Mr McPhail she entreated
his acceptance of the parcel she carried, which contained a large web of linen, of her own spinning,
made long before for the purpose of being presented
to the beloved old man should she ever be permitted to see his face in the flesh once more.

She lived for many years, not only a consistent
character, but an eminently holy Christian.

Will those who read this simple story begin
to pray—

> Lord, show me Myself !
> Lord, show me Thyself !
> Grant me Thy Holy Spirit !
> For Jesus Christ's sake.

THE A.B.C. OF THE GOSPEL

All have sinned, and come short of the glory of
    God.—Rom. iii. 23.

Behold the Lamb of God, which taketh away the
    sin of the world.—John i. 29.

Come unto Me, all ye that labour and are heavy
    laden, and I will give you rest.—Matt. xi. 28.

WILLIAM HUNTER, THE MARTYR BOY

In the year 1554, soon after the accession of Mary ("the Bloody") to the throne of England, there lived in London a lad about nineteen years of age, an apprentice to a silk weaver. His soul had been illumined by divine grace during the controversies of the preceding reign, and he had learned to abhor the falsities of the Papal Church.

When the edict requiring the people to attend mass was published in the name of the bigoted Queen, William's master order him to comply, and to go with him to the church. But the boy replied that he dared not, for he believed that it would be a sin against God for him to countenance such idolatries. And the master drove him from his house.

William walked to the home of his father at Bruntwood, and was kindly received, for his parents loved the boy, feared God, and abhorred Popery.

He sat one day at the door of his father's cottage, poring over a well-worn copy of Tindale's Bible, which his father had laboured long to purchase, and his soul was feeding with joyous relish upon its precious truths, when a priest passed by the door. William, absorbed, did not observe him until he softly approached, looked over his shoulder, and saw the hated volume. The boy started and closed the book. But it was too late. The priest uttered never a word, but scowled portentously, and walked on.

That night William Hunter was thrust into a dungeon. The next day he was taken before Master Justice Brown, who questioned him closely concerning his faith. William would not lie nor would he conceal what he believed. He confessed that he was in heart and soul a Protestant, and that he dared not in conscience attend the mass. He was sent back to his dungeon. His pious father and mother visited him, and encouraged him to persevere in his good confession, even to death. " I am glad, my son," said his mother, " that God has given me such a child, who can find it in his heart to lose his life for Christ's sake.

" Mother," he replied, " for the little pain I shall suffer, which is but short space, Christ hath promised me a crown of joy. May you not be glad of that, mother?"

Then they all kneeled together upon the hard floor of the cell, and prayed that his strength might not fail; that his faith might be victorious.

His parents, as far as they were permitted, supplied his wants and ministered to his comfort. A few of the faithful came to see him, and encouraged him to hold out faithful to the end, and prayed to God with and for him. Others of his acquaintance came and urged him to recant his opinions, to profess or pretend submission to the priests, and not to provoke them to deal more harshly with him. But William in his turn exhorted them to come out from the abomination of Popish superstition and idolatry. The priests, too, expostulated with him, and promised and threatened, but all to no purpose;

he would not abandon his faith in Jesus as a sufficient and only Saviour.

In a few days he was tried, and condemned to be burned to death as a heretic.   They took him back to his dungeon, and after long communion with God in prayer, he lay down and slept.   He dreamed that the stake was set and the faggots piled around it at a place that had been familiar to his boyhood, at the Archery Butts, in the suburbs of the town, and that he stood beside it prepared to die.   And there came to him, in his dream, a robed priest, and offered him life if he would recant and become a faithful son of the Papal Church.   But he thought that he was impelled to bid him go away as a false prophet, and to exhort the people to beware of being seduced by such false doctrines.   He awoke from his dream encouraged and strengthened, believing that grace would aid him to do in reality as he had done in vision.

With the morning dawn, the sheriff came and bade him prepare for the burning.   And when his father had gone, the sheriff's son approached him, and threw his arms around his neck, and wept. " William," said he, " do not be afraid of these men with their bows and bills, who have come to take you to the stake."

" I thank God," said William, " I am not afraid, for I have cast my count what it will cost me already."

As he passed cheerfully out of the prison, he met his father.   The tears were streaming down his face, and all the old man could utter, amid his choking sobs, was, " God be with thee, William, my son ; God be with thee, my son." And William answered, " God be with thee, dear father ! be of good comfort, for I hope we shall soon meet again where we shall be happy."

So they led him to the place where the stake was prepared, and he kneeled upon a faggot and read aloud from the Bible the 51st Psalm. And as he read the words, " The sacrifice of God is a contrite spirit, a contrite and a broken heart thou wilt not despise," William Tyrell, of the Bratches, interrupted him, and said, " Thou liest, thou readest false ; the words are, a humble spirit." " Nay, but the translation saith, a contrite spirit." " The translation is false," quoth Mr Tyrell ; " ye translate books as ye list yourselves, ye heretics." " Well, there is no great difference in the words," said William, and continued his reading.

Then came the sheriff and said to him, " Here is a letter from the Queen, offering thee life if thou wilt yet recant." " No !" said William, " God help me, I cannot recant."

The executioner passed a chain round his body, and fastened him to the stake. " Good people, pray for me," said William. " Pray for thee !" said a priest, " I had as soon pray for a dog." " Well, you have that which you have sought for : I pray God it be not laid to your charge at the last day. I forgive you." " Ah !" said the priest, " I ask no forgiveness from you." " Well, if God forgive you not, my blood will be required at your hands." And then the lad raised his eyes to heaven and prayed, " Son of God, shine upon me." And as he spoke, the sun, over which a dark cloud had floated, suddenly burst as from a veil, and beautifully illumined his countenance.

Then came the priest, whom he had seen in his dream, with a book in his hand to urge him to recant. But the boy, whose soul was nerved to the endurance of martyrdom, waived him away, saying—" Away, thou false prophet. Beware of these men, good people, and come away from their abominations lest ye be partakers of their plagues." " Then," said the priest, " as thou burnest here, so shalt thou burn in hell." But William answered, " Nay, thou false prophet, I shall reign with Jesus in heaven."

And while a voice in the crowd exclaimed, " God have mercy on his soul," and many voices responded, " Amen, amen," they kindled the fire, and the brave Christian boy prayed, " Lord, Lord, receive my spirit ;" his head fell into the smothering smoke, and his soul fled to the loving embrace of the Redeemer, who had purchased it with His own blood.

POOR JOSEPH

Dr Calamy was once preaching in a church in London, when a poor half-witted man, named Joseph, who used to carry burdens through the streets, happened to look at the door. He rested his burden and began to listen. Dr Calamy was preaching from the next—" This is a faithful saying and worthy of all acceptation, that Christ Jesus came into the world to save sinners, of whom I am chief.''

He, in the course of his discourse, spoke of the person of Christ, who He is that came into the world to save sinners—that He was in the beginning with God and was God—that by Him all things were made in heaven and in earth.

Joseph listened, and when the congregation dispersed, he was heard saying to himself: " Joseph never heard this before—that Jesus Christ, the God who made all things—came into the world to save sinners." Bye and bye some person came and said to him: " Yes, Joseph, but have you acted faith?" " Ah, poor Joseph can act nothing," was the reply, " but it is a faithful saying, and worthy of all acceptation that Jesus Christ, the God who made all things, came into this world to save sinners, and why may not poor Joseph be saved?"

At last he became ill. Dr Calamy was sent for, and called on him. When he heard his voice, he said: " Are you the good minister who told me about Jesus Christ coming into the world to save sinners?" Then, taking a little bag of money from under his pillow, he said: " Poor Joseph had set this aside for his old age, but Joseph will never see old age. Take it, and give it to some of Christ's poor people, and tell them that Joseph loves them, and he thinks he loves Jesus Christ for coming into the world to save sinners." This faith of Joseph had hope and love accompanying it. It was not dead faith. Let us show our love to Jesus by opening our hearts to His people.

THE WIGTOWN MARTYRS:

Margaret Lachlison and Margaret Wilson

No chapter in the annals of persecution in Scotland has excited more sympathy and admiration than that recording the last hours on earth of Margaret Lachlison and Margaret Wilson. There have been more tears shed over the martyrdom of Margaret Wilson than over that of any other Scottish martyrdoms. The youth and sex of the martyr, her steadfastness in the face of approaching death——a death which she saw slowly but surely moving up to her as the tide advanced, the refined cruelty of her persecutors in putting the older woman farther out to meet the advancing tide so that her young fellow-witness would see her die, all these go to make up as moving a story as we have on record. John Brown, " the Christian Carrier," shot before the eyes of his wife ; Andrew Hyslop, the shepherd lad returning from the hill, bravely refusing to pull his bonnet over his eyes as he faced his murderers and the Wigtown martyrs all fit in as parts of a damaging indictment, as terrible as any in the chequered records of Scottish history. A determined attempt was made by Sheriff Napier in his " Case for the Crown " to prove that no drowning took place at all but Dr Stewart, Glasserton, in his " History Vindicated " has effectively shattered the Sheriff's arguments.

Margaret Wilson was the daughter of Gilbert Wilson, farmer, Glenvernock. Both his wife and himself were faithful supporters of Episcopacy but their family Margaret, aged 18, Thomas, aged 16, and Agnes, aged 13, were staunch supporters of the Covenanter cause, as represented at that time by the youthful James Renwick who was soon to seal his testimony with his blood.   These young people were asked to take the Test* and requested to attend the services of the curates.   They refused to do both, with the result that they " were searched for, fled, and lived in the wild mountains, bogs, and caves."   Gilbert Wilson's substance was gradually lessened by the inroads made on it by the persecutors who were determined he should suffer for the waywardness of his family.   At length the young people were outlawed, people were forbidden to give them food or shelter.   The cottars and shepherds were required to search for them.   Margaret and Agnes, at length feeling the pangs of hunger left their hiding place and stole down to Wigtown.   They were discovered and apprehended and locked in the Thieves' Hole where the worst of malefactors were their associates.   For six or seven weeks they lay there and in April they were charged with the guilt of Bothwell Brig† and Ayrsmoss.‡   They were sentenced with Margaret Lachlison, a widow, to be " tied to stakes fixed in the sand within the floodmark, and there to stand till the flood overflowed them and drowned them."

* The Test Act was passed in 1681 and required every one taking it to acknowledge that the King was supreme in all matters civil and ecclesiastical.   The stricter Covenanters denied his supremacy in " matters ecclesiastical."

Gilbert Wilson, by a visit to Edinburgh, and a payment of £100, managed to save the life of Agnes.

Margaret Lachlison and Margaret Wilson were taken out of prison to the sands in Wigtown Bay and there tied to stakes to await the onrush of the tide. The older woman (aged 70) was placed further out so that Margaret Wilson would see her die and thus have her resolution broken as her cruel persecutors imagined. When Margaret was asked what she thought of her companion now. " What do I see," was her answer, " but Christ wrestling there ? Think ye that we are the sufferers ? No , it is Christ in us ; for He sends none a warfare on their own charges." Then she opened her Bible and read the 8th Chapter of the Epistle to the Romans, which concludes with " the most triumphant words that were ever uttered by mortal lips."¶ After this she sang her farewell song—it was the 25th Psalm from the 7th verse :

" My sins and faults of youth do thou, O Lord, forget ;

After thy mercy think on me, and for thy goodness great."

(Scottish Metrical Version.)

Many of her relatives lined the banks of the Bladnock, the river flowing into Wigtown Bay, and some of them pled with her to say : " God save the King." " God save him, if He will," she said. " She has said it ! She has said it !" eagerly

shouted some who wished to save her life.   Major
Winram, however, was not satisfied.   He offered
to administer the Abjuration Oath (so hateful to
the Covenanters) to her.   She courageously refused, saying : " I will not, I am one of Christ's
children ; let me go."   Soon the advancing waters
enveloped her and her young life was over.   It
was as sweet to Margaret Wilson in her opening
womanhood as it is to any young girl, but
the crown rights of Christ as King in Sion were
more to her than all else in the world.   While admiring the fortitude of this young witness we must
not overlook the fact that it was the grace that she
received from Heaven that carried her through her
terrible ordeal.   We must not rob God of the
glory that is His while admiring the heroic steadfastness that made her lay down her young life on
the altar to Christ for matters that to thousands of
Scotsmen and Scotswomen to-day, are lighter than
the small dust of the balance.   But Margaret Wilson would have no regrets when her ransomed soul
left her cold body in the Solway Firth and entered
into the happy Home that Christ had prepared for
her.

† The battle of Bothwell Brig was fought in 1679.   The
  Covenanters suffered a disastrous defeat.

‡ The skirmish at Ayrsmoss took place in 1680.   Richard
  Cameron, " the Lion of the Covenant " and his brother
  Michael were killed there.

¶ Open your Bibles and read these wonderful words from
  verses 30-39 and picture to yourself the frail young girl
  tied to the stake and think what the words would mean
  to her.

INTERESTING ANECDOTES

THANKFUL FOR A GOOD APPETITE

A coloured man in U.S.A., who always found a reason for thanking the Lord where others would murmur and complain was one day challenged by those who knew him after he passed through a testing incident.   He was returning home after having purchased a beef-steak.   He stooped down to tie his laces and laying the parcel on the street a dog came along and disappeared with the poor man's dinner.   In telling the story he finished with his usual : " Praise de Lord."   " Do you praise the Lord for the loss of your beef-steak ?" he was asked.   " No sah (sir) ! but 'cause, even if the beef-steak is gone, I still got my appetite left." How many have ever praised the Lord for a good appetite.   Yet what would the finest food be to us if our appetite was gone.   When my young readers feel a good healthy appetite let them not forget what the negro said.

THE BLIND GIRL AND THE BIBLE

Dr Bell relates that a blind girl living in France had for many years perused an embossed Bible with her fingers, but becoming partially paralysed the sense of touch in her fingers was lost. Her agony of mind at the deprivation was great, and in a moment of despair she took up her Bible, bent down, and kissed the open page by way, as she supposed, of a last farewell.　In the act of doing so, to her great surprise and sudden joy, she felt the letters distinctly with her lips, and from that day the door child has thus been reading the Book which is her greatest stay and comfort.—The Bible School, I. 59.

JAMES THE THIRD

Dr Riley of Minneapolis tells the following story in one of his sermons : An invalid mother who devotedly loved her boy called him to her bedside before she died saying, " I want you to be James the Third " and then she proceeded to explain what she meant and told him never to forget her last message to him.　After his mother's death James III, proceeded to College and his name became a subject of curiosity to his fellow students.　One asked if it had anything to do with English history while another suggested that it was probably due to the fact that he was the third child.　To all these suggestions James gave a negative answer.　" What then is the meaning ?" they eagerly asked him and James told them the story of his mother's last message :　" Christ first, my neighbour second, and myself third."　It was good advice from a dying mother and what a different world it would be if we always according to Scripture rule, placed Christ first.

THE ADVENTURES OF A BIBLE

By J. H. TOWNSEND, D.D.

On a dull January afternoon some years ago
—the date of this occurrence is written down in
an old notebook of mine—a young widow was sitting in her drawing-room looking listlessly out of
the window.

It was a fine house in a fashionable Dublin
square ; the room was handsomely furnished, everything indicated comfort and even wealth, but the
possessor looked unhappy.

Mrs Blake was a Roman Catholic, fervent
and conscientious in the practice of her creed ; but
of late her mind had been burdened with the
thought of her sins.   Religious practices, penance,
and even prayers, brought her no relief ; the burden
could not be removed.

She had told her sorrows to her confessor,
and at his bidding had taken up works of charity ;
but, though these things were an interest and for
a while occupied her mind, the sense of her own
sins lay heavy upon her soul.   Her confessor, a
kindly and attractive young priest, gave her full ab-
solution, but his words brought no comfort.

As she sat, musing ; there was a knock at the
hall door, and before she had time to collect her
thoughts a visitor was in the room.

" What shall I do to rouse you and get that
sad look from your face ?"

" Ah, Father John, you are kind and you have done your best, but the burden of which I have told you lies heavy on my heart."

" Listen to me," said he ; " I have made up my mind what you are to do.   There's a man coming to the Rotunda to-morrow night who will make your sides ache with laughing, and you shall go to hear him."

" Oh, Father John—"

" No—not a word ! I won't have any excuse —I enjoin it ! go you will, and go you must."

The young priest explained that a society entertainer, well known at the period, was to appear before a fashionable audience, and that in his opinion this would be the best thing for her.   No protest was of the slightest use ; she could not disobey her spiritual adviser, who had even brought her a ticket for the performance, so the following afternoon saw Mrs Blake at the appointed place, where large placards announced the entertainment which she had been ordered to attend.

The Rotunda had more than one public room under its roof ; there was the great Round Room, the Pillar Room, and one or two more ; there were, moreover, different entrances.   Now, as it happened, Mrs Blake had made a mistake as to the hour of the performance, and instead of the crowd which she would have seen had she come at the right time, she noticed a little string of persons entering the building ; following them she found herself in one of the smaller halls and sat down.

It seemed odd that no one had asked for her ticket, but she concluded that this would be rectified later on.   There was no time for much thought, as almost immediately a gentleman came upon the platform and gave out a hymn.   Then it flashed upon her that she had made some dreadful mistake —she must be in the wrong room, and worst of all, this must be some Protestant meeting into which she had unfortunately found her way.   Mrs Blake was shy and sensitive ; to go out of the place in the sight of all assembled was to her an impossibility. What should she do ?   She determined to slip out at the close of the hymn for by so doing her action would be less likely to attract notice.

This she tried to do, but in her anxiety to be quick she knocked down her umbrella violently, and the noise which it made was so great that many turned round to see the cause.   Poor Mrs Blake, terrified at what she had done, sank into a chair and almost wished that she could fall through the floor.

Now there was a deep silence, and then one voice, that of the man on the platform, was heard in prayer.   She could not help listening, as she had never heard anything like this before ; it was so unlike the " Hail, Marys," and other prayers in her books of devotion.   The man was so reverent, but he seemed so happy as he prayed ; this struck her as most extraordinary.

The prayer ended and the speaker announced that he would read a passage of Scripture on the

" Forgiveness of Sins."   The very subject of all others in the world she longed to hear about! Come what may— let Father John say what he liked or do what he chose—she must listen to this.

The first eighteen verses of the tenth chapter of the Epistle to the Hebrews was read, and the speaker in a simple way expounded the teaching until it became clear as daylight.   The One Sacrifice once offered ; the free and full forgiveness granted to those who ask for it in His name ; this, illustrated by several other passages in the New Testament, formed the subject of the discourse.

As the thirsty ground drinks in the summer rain, so did this poor soul receive these wonderful truths.   She had never heard them before, but now they flowed into her inmost being and she longed to hear more.

The speaker ceased, and after another prayer the meeting broke up.

Mrs Blake felt that this was the opportunity of her life, so, summoning all her courage, she went to the edge of the platform and asked the gentleman whose words he had been reading.

Surprised at such a question he came down and was at once plied with so many inquiries that he offered to write down references for her to study at home.   When, however, he learned that the lady had never possessed a Bible his interest was keenly aroused. " I will lend you mine," he said. " Read the marked passages in the pages which I have turned down, but let me have it back in a few days ; it is the most precious thing I have.''

Mrs Blake thanked him warmly, and hastened home with joy in her heart and a new light in her eye ; how different a being from the disconsolate creature who a couple of hours previously had found her way to the Rotunda.

For the next few days everything was forgotten but her new treasure ; she read and re-read the marked passages and many others too.   The Light shone into her understanding ; the burden, long weighing on her conscience, rolled away into the Open Grave, and the Peace of God filled her heart and mind.

Now the time had come for the Bible to be returned.   Once more she was deep in her new study and so engrossed in thought as not to notice a ring at the hall door.   Someone entered her sitting-room and her confessor stood before her.   He noticed two things ; an embarrassment in her manner, and at the same time a restful calm in her eyes, to which he was a stranger.

'' What has happened to you ?'' said her visitor.   '' I haven't heard how you liked the entertainment, and as I didn't see you at Mass last Sunday I thought you might be ill.''

Taken aback by the suddenness of the whole thing, Mrs Blake lost her self-possession.   She had intended to keep the matter secret for a time at least, but now she was off her guard, and with the simplicity of a child she told the whole story—the mistake of the room, the attempt to go, the words spoken, the book lent, and, last of all, the joy and peace that filled her heart.

With downcast eyes she spoke, but when she glanced up, her spirit froze with terror at the look of the man before her. It was black with rage! Never before had she seen such fury depicted on a face.

" Give me that book !" he said hoarsely.

" It isn't mine !" she cried, vainly attempting to stop him.

" Give it to me," was the reply, " or your soul will be damned eternally; that heretic has nearly got you into hell, and neither he nor you shall ever read the book again."

Seizing it as he spoke, he thrust it into his pocket and, giving her a fearful look, strode out of the room.

The lady sat as if paralysed—she heard the hall door shut, and something in her heart seemed to shut also and to leave her alone in her terror. That awful look searched her through and through ; only those who have been born and brought up in the Church of Rome know the nameless horror which their idea of the power of the priesthood can inspire. Then, too, she thought of the gentleman who had lent her his Bible ; his address was in it, but she could not remember it and knew not where to write.   This was very grievous, but oh! *that look*—it was branded on her memory.

Days passed slowly by, but her visitor, once so welcome, now so dreaded, did not return. Courage began to creep back, and at last, after a fortnight or more had elapsed, Mrs Blake determined to venture upon a visit to him.   She must make one more effort, if not too late, to get the book restored to its rightful owner.

Father John lived at some distance from Mrs Blake's residence, and his house adjoined a convent to which he was confessor.   The door was opened by a nun, who visibly started at the sight of Mrs Blake, and, upon being asked if the priest were at home, her eyes seemed to blaze for a moment, but immediately her face became rigid and her manner cold as she said, " Yes, Father John is at home—he is in this room; will you not come in and see him?"   As she spoke she half led, half pushed, the lady into a room opening off the hall; but as the visitor entered she uttered a piercing shriek, or oh !—horrors of horrors !—*there* was an open coffin, and in it the lifeless form of her confessor.

Before she could recover from the shock, the nun glided up to her and hissed into her ear these words: " He died cursing you: you gave him a Bible, and he told me to tell you that he cursed you—cursed you with his last breath; now go !" And before she well knew what had happened, Mrs Blake was in the street, with the door shut behind her.

Several weeks elapsed.   The breath of spring had passed over the earth, waking leaves and flowers to life and loveliness.   One evening Mrs Blake was sitting alone pondering over the events of the last three or four months.   The joy of pardon was in her heart, she had bought a Bible for herself, and had read it daily.   The old errors in which she had been brought up had been one by one renounced, but there was a sorrow which could not be effaced.   How sad, how ineffably sad, the brief illness and sudden death of that young priest ! His last look ! His last words ! That terrible message !

Why should she have been so blest, brought into the haven of peace, filled with heavenly joy, and he—why should not the same words have brought him a like message ?   It was too awful and was one of those mysteries which could never be explained.   " Why," she said to herself, " should a God of love do this ?"

At this moment the servant ushered into the room a lady who was closely veiled and who stood for a moment irresolute.   Before Mrs Blake could speak, the other said, " You do not know me in this dress, but you will soon recognise me."   With these words she lifted her veil and revealed the face of the nun who had delivered the message of cursing as they stood by the open coffin.

Mrs Blake started back, not knowing what might happen next, but her visitor calmed her fears, adding, " May I sit down and tell you something ?" Having been invited to do so she went on : " I have two things to tell you, and I must be very brief for I am in haste.   First, please, please forgive me for that awful lie of mine; I have asked God's forgiveness, but I beg also for yours.   Father John died blessing you with all his heart.   The day before his death he charged me to tell you that he too had found forgiveness for his sins by that book and that throughout Eternity he would bless you for having brought him to the knowledge of his Saviour. Now, will you forgive me?"

" I will indeed, from the bottom of my heart." gasped the astonished lady; " but why did you say what you did?"

" Because I hated you.   I loved him, and hated you for having sent him to hell as I believed. Now listen.   I felt the strongest desire to read what he had read, and after his funeral I could not resist looking into the book for myself; I was fascinated and read more and more, and I too have found pardon and peace in my Saviour.   I have been studying the Bible for weeks, and now here it is " —producing it as she spoke.   " I have escaped from the convent this evening and will cross to England tonight, but I felt that I must come here to return this Bible, and to tell you that all my life *I, too, shall bless you* for having, through it, taught me how to get forgiveness for my sins.   Goodbye! God bless you! We shall meet in heaven."

A brief farewell, and she had passed out of the house and was gone.

Was it, after all, only a dream ?   A little worn Bible lay on the table before her.   It was no dream, but a glorious reality.   That little book—without a living voice to expound its teaching in two of these cases—had brought three precious souls out of the darkness into light.

Imagine the feelings of its owner when it was restored to him with this wonderful record !   And yet what says the One who sent it on its mission ?

" My word shall not return unto Me void ; but it shall accomplish *that which I please*, and it shall prosper in the thing whereto I sent it."

Reader, *what does your Bible mean for you ?* Jesus said :—

" Verily, verily, I say unto you, he that heareth My word, and believeth on Him that sent Me, hath everlasting life, and shall not come into condemnation ; but is passed from death unto life."   John v. 24.
" This is a faithful saying and worthy of all acceptation, that Christ Jesus came into the world to save sinners."   I Timothy i. 15.

STRANGE FOOTPRINTS OF OUR KING

ISLAND OF SKYE

There was one place in the Island of Skye where the minister used to preach. It was in the parish of Duirinish, in the northern part of the island. A little girl—Mary Bethune—lived there, and was one of his hearers the last time he was there. She was then a girl of about eleven years of age. In listening to him, she was particularly struck with his text. It was in Psalm lxviii, 19-20 —" Blessed be the Lord, who daily loadeth us with benefits, even the God of our salvation. He that is our God is the God of salvation ; and unto God the Lord belong the issues from death."

Under this sermon her young mind began to think, and the two subjects which filled all her thoughts were—death, and the deliverance which God can give.

Her occupation was that of goat-herd, and while out with her flock day after day she kept meditating on these themes ; she found it impossible to do anything else. Whomsoever she met she questioned about God who could deliver from the jaws of death, and when she came home in the evening these were still the subjects of her conversation.

The minister who had so preached to her conscience left the place soon after, and she never saw him again. The minister of her own parish gave her no help ; for, after conversing with her, he agreed with her parents and neighbours in the opinion that the girl's reason was beginning to be unhinged.

However, she was allowed to attend to her duty of keeping the herd of goats; and so she watched for opportunities of putting questions to any she met on the matter that was her great concern.

After continuing thus for some time, finding none qualified to give her information as to how she could get acquainted with that " Jehovah " to whom it belongs " to rescue fully from death " (as it is in the metrical translation of the Gaelic Psalms), and feeling more and more the necessity of being able to say, " Our God is the God of salvation," she came to the conclusion that she could not arrive at the privilege her soul hungered after while remaining in the neighbourhood in which she was. She therefore resolved on prosecuting her inquiry elsewhere.

At that time all necessary commodities not of home growth were procured from Inverness, and conveyed to Skye on horseback.   In her girlish simplicity, Mary Bethune concluded that since so many and such extraordinary things were to be found at Inverness, surely " Jehovah " must be found there too!   At all events, she resolved on proceeding to inquire after the knowledge of the Lord elsewhere, and not to give up the search even if she should need to go as far as Inverness itself.

There were in those days none of the present modes of conveyance from place to place, even in localities more favoured than the districts lying between Skye and the Capital of the Highlands. There were no roads from one part of that country to the other.   There were many rapid rivers and

streams intervening, and none of them had bridges
over them, while also the rapids of Kyle-Rhea flowed
between Skye and the mainland.   But of all that
she took no heed.   Soul-concern had complete
mastery of all her thoughts, and all her affections
too.

When she had her mind made up, she at once
girt herself for the journey.   Her toilet cost her
little thought and less time.   She merely washed
her hands and face in the stream that ran past her,
smoothed her hair as well as she could with her
fingers, and bound it up with a snood.   She threw
her *tonnag* (a square piece of cloth) around her
shoulders, and fastened it across her breast with a
wooden pin or skewer, and then, bareheaded and
barefooted, she proceeded in quest of the object
on which alone her heart was set.

Now, it may be very properly asked, why she
did not ask her parents' consent?   It may also
very likely be suggested, that having thus set out
in disregard of the fifth commandment, she was not
likely to obtain the blessing which her soul was so
very anxious to gain.   But let me here observe that
the fault was not solely hers.   From what is well
known of the state of matters in the place of her
nativity at the time, I plead on her behalf her never
having been instructed in the knowledge of any part
of the truth; and further, her certain knowledge
of what the result would have been had she first
revealed her resolution to those who were her
natural guardians, for assuredly they would have
bound her hand and foot, and confined her as a

maniac.   Hence, in her case, her offence was pardonable, and her resolution was justifiable.   Her remaining where she was would, humanly speaking, have resulted in her growing up in as much ignorance of the true God and of the Saviour as did the kids of her flock.   Accordingly, from hamlet to hamlet did Mary Bethune proceed, questioning all whom she met.   See her now on the way.   Some put her off gruffly ; some ridiculed her as meddling with what was not suitable for a person of her years. The most regarded her as a person under some strange hallucination.

There was, however, no fear of her starving for want of food ; no fear of her being any night without a bed.   The country was not then so much depopulated as it is now.   There were hamlets, consisting of from four or five to perhaps a score of households, within short distances of each other, over the greater part of the way, in places where now no traces of houses are to be seen.   It was, too, the summer season, when everywhere through the hills she would come upon shielings, occupied by persons engaged in tending the flocks and attending to dairy produce.   A poor helpless girl would never fail of meeting with kindness, and sharing in such comforts as the people had.   Indeed, the general belief as to her being out of her mind would draw out pity towards the wanderer, whatever some might have thought of her questions, and even they who would at first have spoken roughly, would soon be melted again, so as to help her forward on her journey.   Still, there is no doubt she must have had trials and hardships by the way not a few.

COMMUNION AT INVERNESS

What time she took to accomplish her weary task is not known ; but the Lord whom she sought after had His blessed eye upon her, ignorant as she still was of Him.   Her way, after crossing Kyle-Rhea, lay through Glenelg ; and after crossing the heights, she made her way through Glenmoriston. She then found herself at Lochness, by the side of which she walked till she arrived at Inverness. She had now reached the only bridge then spanning the River Ness.   It was an oaken bridge, a frail erection, which was carried off some years ago by a flood.   The time was that of the administration of the sacrament of the Lord's Supper in that town. She spoke in her usual strain to those she met, but encountered many strange rebuffs on putting her questions.   At last she was led to address one who at once felt a deep interest in the barefooted bare-headed girl, who had accosted her just as she had many others before.

Mary Bethune observed a person, having the appearance and bearing of a lady, walking along the bridge on her way to the place of worship which she usually attended.   To her she made up.   Repeated disappointments having intensified her earnestness, she called out : *" O lady! is God in this town ? and if so, where shall I find Him ?"* The lady looked at first with amazement, as many others had done on similar occasions—just because an all-important question of this kind is so seldom put. She hesitated a while before replying ; and then, on Mary reiterating the question with still greater earnestness, she replied : '' Yes, God is in this town. Come you with me, and perhaps you may find Him.'' She then took the girl by the hand, walked with her to the church, and led her in to the seat which she herself occupied.

The services of the day having been begun, Mary Bethune was all attention ; and we may suppose her kind friend to have been deeply exercised in prayer for the salvation of the poor friendless child thus providentially thrown on her for protection. The minister engaged in the work that day is said to have been Mr James Calder of Croy, a true man of God, as was his father before him, and as his three sons were after him. He seemed that day to find the declaration of the whole truth an easy matter, and he had one hearer at least who drank in every word he uttered concerning *God*, concerning *the sinner,* and concerning *the Saviour*. And as he became more and more earnest, and more than ordinarily simple and clear while enlarging on the subject in hand, Mary Bethune was enabled clearly to apprehend the truth proclaimed. She could contain herself no longer. She started up, and, clapping her hands, exclaimed : '' *I see Him now; I understand it all now. I have found Him! I have found Him! I have found Him!''*

Many may regard all this as rhapsody. There have been too many instances in which persons who loudly proclaimed their deliverance from ignorance, doubt, and unbelief, have given occasion for scoffers to deride all such experiences as delusion. In Mary Bethune's case, however, that moment in the old Gaelic Church at Inverness proved to be the moment of her spiritual birth.   She soon forgot all her weary wanderings from the western shores of the Isle of Skye.   She now knew One on whom she could lean with assured confidence for time and for eternity.   She realised pardon for the past and the foundation for a good hope for the future.   She might not at that time be able to give such clear answers to questions which might be put to her as she could at a later stage; but she had in her soul a knowledge of the same nature and kind as Anna had when she recognised the promised Messiah in old Simeon's arms in the court of the Temple at Jerusalem.

The first outburst of enraptured feeling over, she sat with all composure during the rest of the discourse, and joined in the service with the congregation.   Mary could now say, " This God is *my own* God, the God of *my* salvation," and she might fully rest on His Providence for all that concerned her welfare in life.   Even should all the people in church pass out without taking any interest in her, she knew that He who kept her and shielded her all the way, and who had that day revealed Himself to her soul, would raise up some friend to act towards her the part of a guardian. She had that, indeed, already; for the kind lady who led her into church could not now part with her.   She conducted her out as she conducted her in.   She brought her to her own house, provided for her wants, and watched over her with a mother's solicitude.

COMMUNION AT DINGWALL

Years passed on.   Mary was evidently growing in grace.   She had found a home and employment in her benefactress' house, and continued in her service till the lady died.   Then she left Inverness and obtained a place of residence in the parish of Croy, where she could enjoy the ministrations of her spiritual instructor in the Lord—Mr James Calder.   Not long, however, after her removal to that parish Mary was called upon to act towards another Skye wanderer the same part that was performed towards herself by the lady whom she met on the bridge on her arrival at Inverness.

You may have heard of the mineral water of Strathpeffer, in the neighbourhood of Dingwall, and may have regarded those waters as if they were only recently discovered.   So far, however, is that from being the case that from time immemorial it appears they were resorted to by certain classes of invalids.   Superstition had long taken advantage of the curative properties of such waters.   When Popery prevailed in the land, and even down to the time we are speaking of, if one went to any well such as those at Strathpeffer he would find all the bushes around covered with rags or handkerchiefs or strips of the garments left by the persons relieved —these being regarded as so many votive offerings commemorative of their thankfulness to the saint who was believed to preside over the healing powers of the wells in question.   It was only at a comparatively recent period that such practices were put down by the power of the Gospel.

To this mineral water at Strathpeffer a farmer's wife from Kilmaluag, in the parish of Kilmuir in Skye, came down, in hopes of recovering from some ailment wherewith she was afflicted.   She was accompanied by a daughter, and they remained for some weeks.   At that time there were three parishes in the neighbourhood highly favoured. The ministers in each were men of God and men of prayer, abounding in works of faith and labours of love.   They had much to do to uproot habits and practices which were the result of ages of superstition and ungodliness.   Among such favoured parishes was that of Dingwall, and in good old Mr Rose's day, and in the days of his predecessor, Mr Mackenzie, the town was the resort—especially at the times of the administration of the Lord's Supper —of great numbers of people.   Many of them were pious persons, while not a few were drawn by mere curiosity.   Among the latter, on the occasion to which our story refers, was the girl from Kilmaluag.   She had seen the Sacrament of the Supper administered in Skye; she had heard preaching, too, both on ordinary and on Sacramental occasions; but she heard now what she had never heard before.   She was struck with amazement. She had begun to discover *what she was* in the sight of the Holy One.

She returned home to her mother under deep conviction of sin, regarding herself as lost, and as being under the curse of God.   But there was a hidden something within, which led her to seek more and more of the truth, however awful her sense of misery was. Nay, further, although herself under a sense of condemnation, she would have her mother go to Dingwall next day along with her, and hear for herself what had so deeply impressed her.

You would perhaps think that her mother would bless the Lord for what she should have regarded as encouraging the hope that her child would now prize the Physician of souls. Instead of that, not knowing herself what it was to be a sinner, she regarded all her daughter's fears as groundless; she, moreover, feared that if her daughter was to go again to Dingwall to hear a sermon, she would be lost to her, or perhaps become crazy. She therefore made preparations for their return to Skye at once; and with this purpose, she replied to her daughter's solicitations by saying:

" Janet, you don't go to Dingwall to-morrow. You and I will stay at home to wash, and to prepare for our journey homewards on Monday."

" Wash to-morrow?" said Janet; " No, no! To-morrow is Sabbath. Neither you nor I should profane that day, and so break the fourth commandment."

But to this exhortation Janet's mother paid no regard. Sabbath found her engaged as she purposed, and she would insist on her daughter joining her in the desecration of the Lord's day.

Janet at first earnestly pleaded with her mother to desist, but it was all to no purpose. She next pleaded for leave to go to Dingwall, but this request was peremptorily refused. The daughter then told her mother that, whatever the consequences might be, she must go to hear the Word of God, and proceeded to arrange her *tonnag* for that purpose.   Seeing this, her wicked mother raised up both her hands, and with fearful oaths imprecated curses on her daughter's head !   She solemnly devoted her to Satan, and charged her at the same time to go away, and never be seen by her again.

Janet screamed bitterly, and ran out of their temporary place of abode.   The people from that neighbourhood by that time had all moved away to Dingwall.   Her first impulse was to go after them ; but after proceeding some way, she felt herself so oppressed with a load of terror that she was compelled to rest.

" What is the use," said she, " of my going to Dingwall ?   There is no hope for me.   I am under the curse of God, and my own mother has devoted me to the enemy.   I can never obtain deliverance.   It is as well for me to turn and direct my steps some other way."

And turn she did.   But the Lord, who, unseen and unknown, had His eye on her, by His own Spirit suggested some recollection of a word she had heard—for read she could not.   She turned again in the direction of Dingwall, and had proceeded some few steps, when the enemy, though formerly foiled, again returned to the assault.   Her former doubts came on with redoubled power, and she walked back again till something else occurred to her which prompted her to "hope against hope." So again she proceeded in the direction of the place where the Gospel was preached.   Matters went on thus for the greater part of the forenoon—Janet sometimes progressing and again returning.

She did reach the outskirts of the congregation at last. We do not know who the minister was who at that special time was speaking; but Janet heard him commending to his hearers the blood of the Cross—holding forth the efficiency of its application for the taking away of guilt, and the removal of a sense of condemnation.   As if he had been specially directed to address Janet personally, she heard him say—" Should you be sensible of the overwhelming load of the curse of God, and your mother's curse along with that, you will find more than enough in this blood for the removal of both, and for rendering you righteous before God."

Janet heard this.   To her it was a word in season.   It calmed the tempest within.   She sat down at the feet of Christ, and heard with diligent attention.   When the congregation was dismissed all went either to their own homes or to the houses of friends, who showed their hospitality to them as strangers coming to the feast.   But Janet had no house to go to; her mother had discarded her; and she might be ready to ask, " What am I to do now?"   The Lord had, however, been graciously revealing Himself to her soul throughout the whole afternoon and evening of that day.   Why, then, should she fear?   Some person might be prompted to show kindness to her; and if not, it was summer, and she could remain outside for one night at least. She heard the sermon intimated for next day, and she would wait for that before she would decide as to where to turn her steps.   Still, who could doubt that, after all, poor Janet would feel something like a weight on her spirit, or rather be conscious of a blank which sadly needed filling up, when she saw the whole congregation gradually melting away, with none to speak a kind word to her?

But, stop! Who is this coming up and approaching Janet Macleod with a kindly smile? This is Mary Bethune now grown up to womanhood, grown in faith and knowledge, and in Christian experience.   She is, moreover, largely acquainted with professing Christians throughout the whole country, and she has come to Dingwall, along with others, expecting a " feast of fat things . . . of wine on the lees well refined." She and they have not been disappointed.   But now the appearance of a Skye girl has attracted her attention.

Janet's dress and manner are almost a new sight to her.   She speaks to her and is convinced by her first word that they are both natives of the same isle.   Her kind inquiries draw out Janet's heart all at once.   The unvarnished tale is soon told; the harrowing horrors and the gracious consolation.   The two are drawn to each other with an influence far more powerful than that of country and kindred.   Janet finds shelter with Mary where she is herself lodged.

From this day forward the two are inseparable.   Mary conducts Janet to the domicile occupied by herself in the parish of Croy.   They continue to sit together under the same minister

(Mr James Calder) till the day of his removal to the Upper Sanctuary.

After Mr Calder's death Mary and Janet found a place of residence, and a ministry which they relished as being profitable to their souls, in the parish of Nigg, in the County of Ross.   Mr Mc-Adam was then newly translated to that charge after the parish had been long under the blight of a minister whose coldness had the effect of scattering the Lord's flock, and of rendering the place of worship a desolation.   Under Mr McAdam's ministry those two godly women continued to sit while they lived, supporting themselves by the labour of their hands, respected in the place, and growing in ripeness for the abode of the just, till at about the age of 80 years they were removed to the enjoyment of the communion of saints above, and the blessedness of uninterrupted fellowship with Him whom they loved so much below.

You may perhaps inquire whether Mary or Janet had any communication with their relatives in Skye ?   Communication by letter was not then so easy as it is now.   Neither of them had learned to write, but Mary had communication with her parents through a namesake of her own who was minister of Alness in the County of Ross.   She went once to her native place and remained there for some time, but, not having the privilege which she had found so delightful in the land of her adoption, she returned again to that district and never afterwards visited the Isle of Skye.

But she and her companion never failed to wrestle together in prayer for the people in their native island ; and I heard a godly minister in Skye, now departed (the Rev. Roderick Macleod) give expression to the complacency he felt in connecting the spiritual influences in each of the parishes whence these women came with the continued and persevering entreaties which they were known to have laid at the foot of the Throne on behalf of their native district.

We may learn, moreover, that a minister may be instrumental for good, while he himself may be denied the privilege of knowing that any good has been done. The minister under whom Mary Bethune's whole soul was roused to seek after the knowledge of the Lord never knew of the effect produced till Mary and he met beyond the grave.

This story is now finished. If the recital may have the effect of stirring up any young person to follow on to know the Lord, I have my reward. If any person, young or old, be incited by the examples here related, to regard everything else as vile in comparison with the knowledge of Christ and Him crucified, I would earnestly bid him God-speed ; let his press on till he know for himself this Saviour " who was delivered for our offences, and was raised again for our justification," till he be " begotten again unto a lively hope through the resurrection of Jesus Christ from the dead."

JOHN ROSS : A STORY FOR THE YOUNG

There was once a little boy who went into a churchyard to look at the tombs ; and, as he walked about, he began to measure the size of the graves, to see how big they were.　He found that many of them were less than himself.　When he saw this, he was much afraid, and began to say to himself, " If I should die soon, and be laid there, what would become of me ?"

Now, I am going to tell you of a little boy, now lying in the churchyard, whose grave is shorter than most of you ; and if you should be taken away as early as he was, what will become of you ?　He was ready to die, for his hope was in Jesus Christ, his Saviour ; but are you as ready as he was ?　Often did he say how glad he would be to depart and " to be with Christ, which is far better."　And often did he speak about Enoch, that holy man, whom God took to himself, and wish that like Enoch, he might walk with God, that God would take him too. Would you, then, my dear children, like to die as soon, and be with Christ, or to remain in this sad, sinful world ?　This good little boy, of whom I am going to tell you, thought it far better to be with his Saviour in heaven ; and one day when he came home from school he told his mother how the teacher had been saying to the scholars how well he would like to see them all when they were grown up : " But, mother," said he, " I'll never be big ; and I wouldn't like to be big ; I would far rather die and go to God."

John Ross was born in Glasgow on the 17th of February, 1828.	He seems to have been one of those whom the Holy Ghost sanctifies from the womb, for before he was two years old, he began to show how much he thought about God.	One day, after family-worship at his grandfather's house, he got hold of the Psalm book, and, laying it upon his knees, began a sort of scream as if trying to imitate the singing in which the family had been engaged.	When asked what he was doing, he answered in the imperfect way of a child so very young, " Me singing to God ; high, high up there : holy, holy God."	Another time, when about the same age, his mother was teaching him the words which say,

" God sees when children dwell in love,
	And marks them for His own."
At hearing these words he stopped, and said : " Will God mark little children like me for His own ?"	His mother told him that God would do so.	" Oh, happy, happy Johnny," he said, " if God would mark him for His own."

At another time, when he was a little older, he was out with his mother in the street, at a time when they were in great poverty.	A gentleman, as they were passing, happening to let fall a half-penny, little Johnny looked eagerly at it, and the gentleman allowed him to pick it up and keep it. As soon as he had passed, Johnny said : " Mother, was you praying as we were walking along ?" " What makes you ask that ?" said his mother. " Because," said he, " that half-penny came from heaven.	It was God that sent it.	He saw it in the gentleman's pocket, and He said, ' That half-penny is for Johnny,' and so the gentleman could not lift it.'' Now, does not this show how little Johnny, although he was scarcely five years old at that time, had learned to put his trust in God as His heavenly Father, and to know that everything came from Him alone ? Have you learned this ?

As he grew older, this work of God's Spirit in his heart became more remarkable.   In all that he spoke and did, he showed that, young as he was, he had become a new creature in Christ Jesus.   He was not only free from the outward sins which are common amongst children, but he could not bear the idea of offending God.   On one occasion he said : '' It's just like to break my heart to see people sinning against God.''   On another, he came into the house much agitated, and evidently in great distress.   His mother asked him if anyone had been hurting him.   He answered :   '' Oh, mother, they'll let none of the Persons of the Godhead alone ; as I came along the street just now, I heard a person swearing by the Holy Ghost.''   Though he was of a happy, cheerful, contented disposition, he would often seem sad for some time after hearing people swear on the street.   On these occasions he would take his pencil and write : '' Holy, holy, holy, Lord God Almighty.''   If he found a piece of paper on the street with God's name upon it, he would lift it up and fold it carefully and bring it home.   And often he would say, '' How grieved am I to see His holy name despised !''

He had a remarkable sense of God's being present everywhere with us, hearing all our prayers and marking all we do.   One day his neighbour's servant had been speaking to him about the uselessness of praying to God, and telling him it was nonsense.   When he came home he said: " Oh, mother, do you know what —— has been saying? She says its all nonsense to pray to God, and He everywhere present, and hears all that we say." One morning, being much distressed at his father's conduct the night before, he told him: " God sees everything you do, and marks down all your thoughts.   I would not take the whole world and make Him angry with me: but unless we have a clean heart, we cannot serve Him; for God is a Spirit and they that worship Him must worship Him in spirit and in truth.   I must write something behind the outer-door, and you must read it when you go out and when you come in, and, if you read it, it will keep you from much sin."   Accordingly, he took his pencil and wrote the following verse:

" The Lord who made the ear of man,
    Must needs hear all of right,
He made the eye, all things must then
    Be plain in His clear sight."

The person who writes this account of Johnny has been at his house and seen this verse which he wrote with his own little hand upon the wall of his father's house; and when he saw it he wondered at the grace of God that had put such things into the heart of a child not eight years old!   I have also seen several of Johnny's little books, which are all written over with some pious sentences, or good words, or verses of hymns.   I have one of these books beside me just now while I am writing to you, and on its boards I find the following words written: " Bible is true and no lie—Kirk the best place you go to—holy book—the Bible, the best book—the Lord my pasture shall prepare, and feed me with a shepherd's care."

I have seen many of your books, many hundred books, which children have been reading; and I have seen many marks upon them; but I have never seen any like this of little Johnny's. What then makes the difference between him and you? What made him love these things so well when you are so careless about them? It was the Lord, the Spirit, that had given him a new heart, and made him love these things. And to show you still more how he loved these things, I shall tell you another story about him. One time, after speaking to his father about his conduct, he took a piece of paper and wrote upon it the ten commandments, and then hung it up where his father used to shave himself, and told him to read what God had commanded, every day, when he rose from his bed. And standing, looking earnestly at the paper which he had hung up, he said: " Oh, how love I Thy law! It is my study all the day." At another time, when sitting at the fireside reading his Bible, he came to that passage which says: " If the Son therefore shall make you free, ye shall be free indeed." Upon reading this he turned round and said to his father, who was sitting near him: " Father, you're not free, you're the slave of sin; but then," said he, " I'm free, I'm God's free-boy." On reading one day about Daniel in the lions' den, he said : " God shut the lions' months—yes ; and their eyes too—they never saw him ; they never knew he was there."

He was so remarkably simple and free from guile, so much so that he seemed quite indifferent in regard to the things of the world.   He could not bear anything that had the appearance of a lie, and whenever he found any of his companions telling a falsehood, he would leave their company altogether.   There was one boy with whom he was very intimate, and who used often to meet him after he came from school.   This boy began one day to boast of something he had done, which boast Johnny at once saw to be a lie.   Upon this he told him that he must never again come to his house, and that he would have nothing more to do with him till he was a better boy.   His mother asked him how he would know he was a better boy.   He said that he would soon see some marks which would show him that he was better.   " And what marks will you know it by ?"   " I think," said he, " the biggest mark will be that he loves God."   There is another very striking fact which shows not only that he hated lying, but how anxious he was to prevent others from lying   As his appetite for food was very small, and as he ate but little at meals, his mother used often to put a piece of dyed loaf into his pocket, that he might eat it while in the school. Some wicked boys, finding this out, one day came to him and told him that if he did not give them his dyed loaf, they would tell his master some stories about him.   Upon his mother asking him what he did, he told her that he gave them his dyed loaf,

" for," said he, " mother, it was far better for me to give it to them, than to have them telling lies and sinning against God."

Whenever he found any of his companions telling a lie, he not only separated from them, but always reproved them, and told them that they reminded him af Ananias and Sapphira, and were so like the devil. When he heard of any of them being guilty of sin, he used to take a piece of paper and write down the commandment which they had broken, and then go and hand it in at the door of their house.

He was very fond of school, and attended most regularly, both on week-days and on Sabbath evenings. Every day, when he returned from school, he took his Bible, and having sung a few verses of a Psalm, he prayed that all he had been learning at school might be blessed to him. He was very careful to understand all that he learnt, and could never be content till he had not only understood the words which he read, but the doctrines which he was taught. The words which he made use of were remarkably correct and much beyond what could have been expected from his years. One time, being grieved at his father for swearing, he advised him to go and pray. His father said he would go some other time. He clasped his little hands in evident distress, and said, " Procrastination?—Oh, you will procrastinate till time is done, and what will become of you then?" He was very anxious to have the meaning of justification and sanctification explained to him, and seemed often thinking about it. One morning, before he

went to school, when speaking about the sufferings
of Christ, he said, " I often wonder how God could
die upon the cross.   How was it, mother?"   His
mother told him that He took our nature into union
with the divine nature, and that, though as God He
could not suffer, He suffered as man.   " Oh,"
said he, " that is just it," and after a little while
he said, " My finite capacity cannot comprehend
it."   Speaking of that passage in the Epistle to
the Ephesians which speaks of Christians growing
up into the stature of perfect men in Christ, he
said that what he would like to grow for would be
that he might grow up unto that stature.   And
then he asked, " Mother, can a little boy grow up
into a perfect man in Christ?"   On being told
that he could, he said he was glad, for then he would
not need to wait till he was grown-up.

     He was fond above all things of his Bible, and
would always be reading it.   He liked much to
read the first chapter of Genesis, about the creation
of all things ; and one Sabbath morning his mother
noticed he had read it over four or five times before
breakfast.   She spoke to him about it, and he
told her how much he liked to read it.   " Oh,
mother," he said " my heart grows big when I
read it, and these words, ' God said, let there be
light, and there was light ;' then, repeating the
words and laying the emphasis on " was ;" " and
there ' was ' light, for whatsoever God says must
be."   He was very fond of speaking about the
Resurrection and the second coming of Christ, and
on such occasions his face used to become quite
flushed with animation.   " I shall be a King and

a Priest," he would say, " on that day, and I shall
have a glorious crown put upon my head."

He was very fond of the Sabbath Day, and
used to express horror at any profanation of it in
the strongest way.   One day, reproving his father
for something of this kind, he said—" On this day
Christ rose from the dead, and after Him suffering
and dying to take away our sins, you would dare
to profane His holy day ; it frights me to look at
you ; and besides, what an example you are setting
before me.   God is very angry at you."   His
father said—" Are you not ashamed to speak to
your father in that way ?" He said :—

> " I'm not ashamed to own my Lord,
>   Or to defend His cause."

One night his father came home much intoxicated,
and after he went to bed, little Johnny was sitting
thoughtfully at the fireside.   After a little
he turned round and said to his mother—" Mother,
I was just thinking what a fool the devil is torment-
ing us in this way, when he knows that he only gives
us an errand to God every time he sends my father
home in that state."

One day, coming home from school, he said
that a bad boy had been pushing at him during
prayer.   His mother said that none prayed but the
master.   He answered—" But our mind prays,
and when the teacher is done, my mind says, ' O
Lord, hear Mr——and make us all holy.' "   He
had a great dread of offending God, and it was
evident that his faith wrought by love.   He often
expressed his thankfulness to God for temporal

mercies, and never would eat a morsel without asking a blessing.

It was his practice every morning to take his Bible into the closet where he slept, and sing some verses of a Psalm, then read a chapter, and afterwards pray. He often prayed fervently for his father. As soon as he returned from school he took his Bible again, and read and sang and asked a blessing upon what he had been learning at school. He spent much of his time during the day in singing God's praises. He was never idle, and often employed himself in drawing. On his mother noticing ejaculations of praise written here and there, she said to him one day—" You should not do the like of that." He said—" When I think of God, I forget, and just write down what I think." He was fond of astronomy, and on reading the discoveries made by it, he would say—" What a great and glorious God we have! "

On coming home from church on that day when he took his last illness, he complained of a pain in his back. His mother told him he must stay at home from the Sabbath School that night. He said he would go and hear about Christ. He came home very ill, with a bad pain in his head, which continued, gradually getting worse till Saturday. On Saturday forenoon he cried out, " My God, my own God, help my head or take me to heaven," and then taking his mother's hand, he told her he was dying. She asked him if he was afraid to die. He said, " No, he wished to die, if it was God's will," adding that sweet word, " Sleep in Jesus makes me happy when I think on the grave." Though he had formerly a great aversion to medicine, he now said he would take whatever the doctor ordered for him, in case God would be angry with him for refusing it ; but he said that he felt he could never recover. On Sabbath morning, while rather quiet, he cried out—

" This is the day that Christ arose—
So early from the dead."

" He lay in the grave," said he, " and rose for my justification. His own Word says it, and it makes me all glad." On Monday he asked for his mother to send for his teacher. He said he loved him much, and when asked why he loved him, he said, " Because he loves God, and I love every one who loves Him." He was particularly pleased at his teacher's visits, and at one time said—" How glad I am that he is not tired of coming to see me ; how happy he and I will be in heaven for ever !"

He asked one day—" What day of the month is this ?" On being told it was the tenth, he said —" That good lady that brings the tracts is not come ; I would like to see her before I die ; I know she is a child of God : she goes about to see and make bad people good. Thank her mother, when I die, and tell her I'll see her in heaven. My mind loves her for giving us the tracts : tell her to continue to give the tracts, that wicked people may be the better of them." He used to keep and collect together the monthly tracts as they were delivered, and he took great delight in showing them to any person who visited the house. He was anxious also to pay for the tracts which he relished so much, and had resolved on collecting five shillings for this purpose, but his means were so slender that he died before he collected this sum.

He once said—" I think, mother, I belong to Him." His mother said—" To whom?" He answered—" To God—the faculties of my soul, my understanding, my will, my affections: I'm God's boy altogether, mother. Will you tell everybody what justification and sanctification is? I wish the whole world would love God and serve Him." His patience and resignation were most remarkable. In great pain, he said one day— " How I thank God for this sore head, for it was sent to take me to heaven." One time, when expressing his conviction that he would go to heaven, he was told that all who died did not go to heaven. He said—" I know that, but all for whom Christ died go there; and He died for me." At another time he said—" I must sing a louder song in heaven than the holy angels." His mother asked him how. He said—" My song will be to Him who washed me from my sins in His own blood. O how I love him!"

At one time he seemed to get quite insensible so as not to notice anything. When he revived again, his mother asked him if he felt anything when he was in that state. He said he did, though he could not utter a word. " My tongue couldn't speak," he said, " but my mind was speaking all the time, and saying, O Lord, send Thy Spirit into my heart."

He admonished his father to beware of provoking God, and in a little after he said to him—

" Trust in God, father, that is what you should do, but the wicked cannot trust in God.   If you do not seek Him you shall never see me more till I be a witness against you at the last day."   On the Monday before his death, he said—" I have got no sleep for two weeks, with this awful pain in my head, but I will get a sound sleep soon."   The pain was so severe that he never slept ten minutes at once during his illness, but he never uttered a discontented word the whole time.   His head having been blistered one day, when dressing it, his mother said—" My afflicted boy!"   He immediately replied—" Your happy boy! Mother, you shall soon see that head with a crown of glory up it.   This was on Monday afternoon.   He then asked if it was five o'clock.   His mother said it was after four.   He continued to ask repeatedly if it was five, and said he was to be well at five.   He then said, " Three Persons in the Godhead—God the Father made and preserved me; God the Son came into the world and died for me; God the Holy Spirit came into my heart, and made me love God and hate sin."   After this he spoke but little, he got so weak, till exactly at five o'clock he slept in Jesus, on Tuesday evening, the 16th of August 1836, being just about eight years old.

LIONEL THOMSON, OBAN

This dear little boy was only a little over five years of age when he died.   He had gone to school at the end of last summer, and was making good progress with his lessons.   But his love for the Bible captivated his youthful mind.   In fact, he was like the nobleman who sold everything he had

to become possessor of the greatest treasure of all.
Little Lionel sold his childish pleasures and went
away by himself to have the Bible read to him.

Both his parents belong to Lewis.   Lionel went
there some time before his mother's father died.
His chief anticipation in going to Lewis was that
his *seanair* (grandfather) would read the Bible to
him.

Ever since he could make his thoughts understood, it was quite evident that this child was not
like ordinary children.   His mind seemed over-
shadowed by the reality of something beyond the
things of time, and he began to ask solemn and
wonderful questions.

When he heard Bible stories read to him, he
seemed to conclude that it was through this Book
an answer could be found to his many questions.
His love for the Bible became so intense that he
would listen for hours to hear it read to him, and
this at his own earnest request.   But he did not
worship the Bible as a book.   The secret of his
love for it lay in the fact that he had found Jesus
in it.   Its central figure to him was not Joseph,
Moses, David, nor any of the saints, but Jesus, and
he fell in love with Jesus.   A few days before he
died he was speaking about the Cross on which
Jesus died.   Yet to him, as to the Apostle Paul,
Jesus was not dead.   He was alive and in heaven.
This knowledge led him to think and talk about
heaven.   And as Jesus was to him the central
figure in the Bible, so now towards the close of his
short life, Jesus was the central figure in heaven.
As he formerly, and to the end, loved to have the

Bible read to him, that he might *know* more about
Jesus, so towards the end of his life he longed to go
to heaven to *see* Jesus and be with Him forever.

He had everything a boy of his age would wish
to have in his home and among his neighbours.
Everyone loved him, and his health was perfect.
Yet he was, from time to time, expressing a longing
desire to go to heaven.   When he was asked why
he talked like that : " Did he wish to leave his
father and mother and the children who loved him
so much ?"   His reply was that he loved them all
very much, but that he loved Jesus more.   A few
days before he died, he was heard to say, in holding
up his little hands, " Oh, take me to heaven now."
Jesus heard His lamb's prayer, and took him to
heaven to be with Himself.

He seemed to think that Jesus would come for
him, for after returning from school one evening
shortly before the end came, he said to a neighbour who loved him and to whom he used to speak
freely about Jesus, " Maybe I will not be going to
school for very long now, and then my little sister
can get my books."   His death came in the following wonderful manner.   As he and his older
brother left their home to return to school after
dinner, a gust of wind knocked Lionel down outside
their own gate.   In falling he struck his head
against the kerb, and the side of his head was badly
cut.   He returned into the house quite conscious.
It was decided to take him to the Hospital and have
the wound stitched.   His parents went with him,
and he was himself brave and cheerful.   The
doctors told his parents to wait and that in a quarter

of an hour they would have the wound dressed. They gave him an anaesthetic, but before they got the wound stitched Lionel passed away to be for ever with Jesus whom he longed to see.

We are apt to think, like the disciples of old, that children should not be brought to the Saviour. Maybe it is easier, humanly speaking, for the Holy Spirit, Who alone glorifies Christ, to communicate saving knowledge to children than to adults. In any case, we know that the Bible, from beginning to end, gives a wonderful place to children. The Psalms refer to babes and sucklings praising God. The Saviour quotes this Psalm when the children in the temple were singing His own praise. The place the Gospels give to children is also wonderful. That they were members of the visible Church under the New Testament is evident, for we find Paul adressing them as such and quoting the special commandment in the Decalogue which belonged to them. And he points out that the children's commandment is the only one that has a promise attached to it.

It is unnatural and unscriptural to exclude the children from the visible Church. The blessed Redeemer still takes them up in His arms and blesses them. The more we think of Lionel Thomson, his love for the Bible, his longing to go to heaven to see Jesus Whom he loved so much, the more convinced we are of this.

Our dear Lionel was buried on the 12th January, 1952, amid great sorrow and deep sympathy with his bereaved parents.

LETTERS TO SEEKING SOULS

Dear Friend,

According to promise, I sit down to talk with you a little concerning the great things of an eternal world.   How kind it is in God that He has given us such an easy way of communicating our thoughts, even at a distance !

My only reason for writing to you is, that I may direct your soul to Jesus, the sinner's friend. '' This man receiveth sinners.''   I would wish much to know that you were truly united to Christ, and then, come life, come death, you will be truly and eternally happy.   Do you think you have been convinced of sin ?   This is the Holy Spirit's work, and His first work upon the soul.   (John 16, v. 8 ; Acts 2, v. 37, and 16 v. 29, 30).   If you did not know your body was dangerously ill, you would never have sent for your physician ; and so you will never go to Christ, the heavenly Physician, unless you feel that your soul is sick even unto death. Oh ! pray for deep discoveries of your real state by nature and by practice.   The world will say you are an innocent and harmless girl ; do not believe them. The world is a liar.

PRAY TO KNOW THE WORTH OF YOUR SOUL

Have you seen yourself vile, as Job saw himself ?—Job 40, v. 3 and 4 ; and 42, v. 5, 6 ; undone, as Isaiah saw himself ?—Isaiah 6, v. 1 and 5. Have you experienced anything like Psalm 51 ?   I

do not wish you to feign humility before God, nor
to use expressions of self-abhorrence, which you do
not feel; but oh pray that the Holy Spirit may let
you see the very reality of your natural conditions
before God! I seldom get more than a glance at
the true state of my soul in its naked self. But
when I do, then I see that I am wretched, and miser-
able, and poor, and blind, and naked.—Revelation
3, v. 17. I believe every member of our body has
been a servant of sin—Romans 3, v. 13, 18—
throat, tongue, lips, mouth, feet, eyes. Every
faculty of our mind is polluted.—Genesis 6, v. 5.

Besides, you have long neglected the great
salvation; you have been gainsaying and dis-
obedient. Oh that you were brought to pass sentence on yourself, guilty of all! Hear what a dear
believer writes of himself: " My wickedness, as I
am in myself, has long appeared to me perfectly
ineffable, and swallowing up all thought and imag-
ination, like an infinite deluge, or mountains over
my head. I know not how to express better what
my sins appear to me to be, than by heaping infinite
upon infinite, and multiplying infinite by infinite.
When I look into my heart and take a view of my
wickedness, it looks like an abyss infinitely deep,
and yet it seems to me that my conviction of sin is
exceeding small and faint."

Perhaps you will ask, why do you wish me to
have such a discovery of my lost condition? I
answer, that you may be broken off from all schemes
of self-righteousness; that you may never look into
your poor guilty soul to recommend you to God;

and that you may joyfully accept of the Lord Jesus Christ, who obeyed and died for sinners.   Oh that your heart may cleave to Christ! May you forsake all, and follow Jesus Christ.

COUNT EVERYTHING LOSS FOR THE EXCELLENCY OF THE KNOWLEDGE OF CHRIST

You never will stand righteous before God in yourself.   You are welcome this day to stand righteous before God in Jesus.   Pray over Philippians 3, v. 7,9.   I will try and pray for you.

Grace be with you.

Your friend in Jesus,

Robert Murray M'Cheyne.

Dundee, 1841.

TO A YOUNG BOY ANXIOUS ABOUT HIS SOUL

My Dear Boy,

I was very glad to receive your kind note, and am glad to send you a short line in return, although my time is much taken up.   You are very dear to me, because your soul is precious; and if you are ever brought to Jesus, washed and justified, you will praise Him more sweetly than an angel of light. I was riding among the snow to-day, where no foot had trodden, and it was pure, pure white; and I thought again and again of that verse:

" Wash me, and I shall be whiter than snow."

That is a sweet prayer—make it your own. Often go alone and look up to Jesus, who died to wash us from our sins, and say, " Wash me." (Psalm 51, v. 7). Amelia Geddie was one day dressed in a new white frock, with red ribbons in her bonnet, and someone said to her, " No doubt you will think yourself very trim and clean?" " Ah! no," she said, " I will never think that until I have the fine robe of my Redeemer's righteousness put upon me."

I am glad, my dear boy, you think that God is afflicting you to bring you to Himself. It is really for this that He smites you. His heart, His hand and His rod are all inscribed with love. But then, see that He does bring you to Himself. Do not delay. The lake of fire and brimstone stretches beneath every soul that lives in sin. " There is no peace, saith my God, to the wicked." If the Lord Jesus would but draw the curtain and let you see His own fair face, and His wounded side, and how there is room for the guiltiest sinner in Him, you would be drawn to Jesus with the cords of love.

I was preaching in Perth last Sabbath. When I came out, a little girl came up to me, I think about three or four years old. She wanted to hear of the way to be saved. Her mother said he had been crying the whole night before about her soul, and would take no comfort till she should find Jesus.

Oh! pray that the same Spirit may waken you. Remember Johnnie, you once wept for your soul, too, and prayed and sought Jesus. Have you found him? or have you looked back, like Lot's wife, and become a hard, cold pillar of salt? Awake again, and call upon the name of the Lord. Your time may be short, God only knows. The longest life-time is short enough. It is all that is given you to be converted in. They are the happiest who are brought soonest to the bosom of Jesus.

Write me again. At present I must draw to a close. Give my kindest remembrances to your Mamma, and to A. when you write. Tell him to write me. May you all meet at the table of Jesus above; and may I be there, too, a sinner saved by grace.

Ever yours,

Robert M. M'Cheyne.

Collace, January 27th, 1842.

" Man's chief end is to glorify God, and to enjoy him forever."

" The Spirit applieth to us the redemption purchased by Christ, by working faith in us, and thereby uniting us to Christ in our effectual calling."

" Effectual calling is the work of God's Spirit, whereby, convincing us of our sin and misery, enlightening our minds in the knowledge of Christ, and renewing our wills, he doth persuade and enable us to embrace Jesus Christ, freely offered to us in the gospel."

Answers to questions, numbers 1, 30 and 31 in the " Shorter Catechism " by the Assembly of Divines at Westminster.

" Lord, who shall stand, if thou, O Lord,
      should'st mark iniquity?
But yet with thee forgiveness is,
      that fear'd thou mayest be."

      —Psalm 130, v. 3, 4 (Metrical).

" Who can his errors understand?
      O cleanse thou me within
From secret faults.   Thy servant keep
      from all presumptuous sin."

      —Psalm 19, v. 12, 13.

The experience of the godly John Bunyan
(Author of " The Pilgrims Progress ") after
years of service to God:—

" I find to this day seven abominations in my
heart; (1) Inclinings to unbelief.   (2) Suddenly
to forget the love and mercy that Christ mani-
festeth.   (3) A leaning to the works of the law.
(4) Wanderings and coldness in prayer.   (5) To
forget to watch for that I pray for.   (6) Apt to
murmur because I have no more, and yet ready to
abuse what I have.   (7) I can do none of those
things which God commands me, but my corrup-
tions will thrust in themselves.   ' When I would
do good, evil is present with me.' "

" These things I continually see and feel,
and am afflicted and oppressed with; yet the Wis-
dom of God doth order them for my good.   (1)
They make me abhor myself.   (2) They keep me
from trusting my heart.   (3) They convince me of
the insufficiency of all inherent righteousness.   (4)
They show me the necessity of fleeing to Jesus.   (5)
They press me to pray unto God.   (6) They show

me the need I have to watch and be sober.   (7)
And provoke me to look to God, through Christ,
to help me, and carry me through this world."

—from " Grace Abounding to the Chief of
Sinners."

" O taste and see that God is good :
　　who trusts in him is bless'd.
Fear God his saints : none that him fear
　　shall be with want oppress'd.

The lions young may hungry be,
　　and they may lack their food :
But they that truly seek the Lord
　　shall not lack any good.

O children, hither do ye come,
　　and unto me give ear ;
I shall you teach to understand
　　how ye the Lord should fear."

　　　　　　　　　—Psalm 34, v. 8 - 11.

They shall be brought with gladness great,
　　and mirth on every side,
Into the palace of the King,
　　And there they shall abide.

Instead of those thy fathers dear,
　　thy children thou mays't take,
And in all places of the earth
　　them noble princes make.

Thy name remember'd I will make
　　through ages all to be :
The people therefore evermore
　　shall praises give to thee.

　　　　　　　　　—Psalm 45, v. 15 - 17.

OTHER PROFITABLE LITERATURE AVAILABLE

" THE YOUNG PEOPLE'S MAGAZINE."   Issued
Monthly at 6d per copy (8d by post).   Annual
Subscription 8s 6d.

" THE CHRISTIAN'S GREAT INTEREST,"
William Guthrie, at 5s 6d per copy.

ree Presbyterian Church

" THE LIFE OF ... Magazine ... consists of a section for
D.D. ...to read; it is Reformed; it is sometimes forth-
...has topical comment; has biographical
" THE WESTM... ...k reviews; sermons and other articles.
including th...
Sum of S...
Family ...has a section for Young People. In this section
Script...ill find the Editor's Page with comment; helpful
...les on understanding the Scriptures and also the
" THE ...tory of Christianity; and a section given to Scripture
...cises for Primary to Senior age groups.
cov...

...lished monthly and costs 22 pence per copy,
Book List and other Tracts,

All obtainable from—
> The Publications Treasurer,
> Palmerston Villa,
> 4 Millburn Road,
> Inverness, Scotland.

TE DUE

Epidemiology: A Very Short Introduction

Very Short Introductions available now:

For more information visit our web site:
www.oup.co.uk/general/vsi/